SO-AZW-003

BOB VOILAND

Bike Enterprises: Lakewood, Colorado

© 1994 by Bob Voiland

Cover design: Bob Schram/Bookends

Library of Congress Cataloging-in-Publication Data

Voiland, Bob
     Hurt City / by Bob Voiland
        p.   cm.
     Includes index.
     ISBN 0-9639673-0-4
     1. Bicycle touring—United States.   2. Cyclists—United States—
Biography.   3. Bicycles—Equipment and supplies.   I. Title.
GV1045.V65   1994
796.6′4′09794—dc20   93-47643
                                                                              CIP

1   2   3   4   5   6   7   8   9

Printed in the United States of America by
Johnson Printing Company
1880 South 57th Court
Boulder, Colorado 80301

For Anne, who kept picking me up.

CONTENTS

PREFACE

Someone once said that a person might consider himself blessed if during his lifetime he had one truly good friend, two at the most. I cannot imagine qualifying rules so stringent and callous that only one or two individuals would survive the appraisal.

Do not be troubled by the appearance of a strange name on the following pages. The name is there for the purpose of authenticity and in many instances identifies someone who came to be an enduring friend. Four of these keep reappearing in this story. They are identified by first name only: Anne, Arch, Woody, and Bud.

Bob Voiland

CHAPTER 1

THE DESTROYER

Anne gave me the bike for my birthday twenty-nine years ago. She bought it from a kid in the neighborhood. The bicycle was a loving gift from a wife more in tune with my needs than I was. It was a huge beautiful ten speed, painted bright orange with matching colored plastic tape on the dropped handlebars. It had stem-mounted shifters, brake lever extensions, kick stand, and toe clips. But the bike was woefully heavy. It weighed forty pounds, almost twice that of a quality bicycle today.

The first thing I did before riding was remove the toe clips. I did not want to be attached to that assembly of metal in any way if I had to bail out in a hurry. After some tentative loops in and out of our driveway, I ventured onto the streets. The bicycle seemed awfully big, but I was big too, so maybe the match was reasonable.

However, for several years I didn't ride much. If I made a round trip from my home in Lakewood, Colorado, to Golden—about twelve miles—my body announced emphatically that the activity should cease. Most of all, my rear end hurt. The only non-standard component on the bike was a hard leather Brooks saddle. The seat was not matched to my anatomy. I visited a bike shop to discuss this problem and they immediately made me an offer for the saddle. With its value thus enhanced, I decided to endure the contours of the leather. With five- and ten-mile rides, it just didn't work. I began to refer to the bike as the Destroyer.

In the summer of 1977, I was allowed a three-month sabbatical from work, which deserved a meaningful activity. I decided to go on a bicycle tour of the Colorado mountains. I had some suspicion that my body might be ill-equipped for this venture, so I adopted a training program. I attached the toe clips and learned to deal with them. Anne and I transported the Destroyer to Estes Park in a car and I rode from our cabin to Boulder, a distance of about forty miles. I could tolerate the saddle and wasn't overtired, so I figured I was ready. I neglected to consider that the ride involved a drop in elevation of about three thousand feet.

Jon Giltner lifted the bike which I had proudly displayed in our Boulder office. "Bob," he announced, "if you can ride this thing in the mountains, you can ride anything, anywhere. You're going to hurt a lot. Don't be afraid to eat some aspirin, even while you're riding. It can't do any harm."

I decided to embark at noon so that the climb west out of Lakewood would be limited during the first day. I would try to get past Idaho Springs, to the town of Empire. It's obvious now that I knew just enough to be dangerous. I had a small hiker's waist pack tied to the handlebars with string. Inside was a jogging suit, spare T-shirt, socks, shorts, and windbreaker. I also had my billfold with the essential plastic, water bottle, cable lock, and a vial of root beer flavored dextrose tablets. I wore a helmet, a three-quarter-inch square mirror on my sunglasses, biker's gloves, T-shirt, swimming suit with athletic supporter (a big mistake), socks, and tennis shoes. It is now grievously apparent what I did not have. I had no camping gear, rain gear, food, tools, tubes, pump, or patchkit. If there was a flat or any sort of mechanical problem, it was all over. I would have to be rescued.

My route was U.S. 6, next to Clear Creek. I walked the bike through all the tunnels, on a gravel path. I arrived in Empire sweating but I felt reasonably good. After looking for a motel, which was nonexistent, I rode a block north of the highway to the historic Peck House and secured lodging. I struck my head against the ceiling while carrying my bike upstairs and was glad that I was wearing a helmet. A shower and gourmet dinner made me feel better, but my leg muscles were starting to complain. Sleep was fitful.

After breakfast in a restaurant "downtown," I was dismayed to discover that someone had rifled the pack on my locked bicycle. Nothing was stolen, but this early lesson taught me that a bike, locked or unlocked, should be constantly visible. The climb west from Empire was severe and I must have shown the effects early. Some workmen looked at me and shook their heads as I approached the first switchback below Berthoud Pass. I had vowed to save the largest ring on the freewheel for an emergency, but I was in trouble soon and had to shift into granny.

"This is the dumbest thing I ever did," I said aloud. "In two months I'll be fifty. What am I doing here? This is the dumbest . . ."

I could not believe the effort it took to force the bike up that grade. I stopped often, embarrassed to look at motorists as they passed. I stared off into the trees and tried to look cool. Early on I was determined not to walk and push the bike, but that resolve soon failed. I would intermittently ride, walk, or stand and gasp. I did ride the last half mile to the summit, at 11,315 feet, because I expected tourists to be parked there. They were. I passed and tried to grin.

I needed food desperately, but was afraid that I would quickly lose anything that I ate. I went in a restaurant across from the ski lift terminal and asked if they had any soup. Since that was unavailable, I attacked a quart of orange juice. Some strength gathered. When I returned to the bike, I saw a pile of granular rubber on top of the left chainstay. I didn't know how long the rear tire had been rubbing against the rim. This was corrected quickly by realigning the wheel. It did not dawn on me that I was fortunate to have quick-release hubs.

The ride down the north side of Berthoud Pass was not the fun it should have been. I was too shaky to go all out, so I braked a lot while sitting erect. Also, my body was hurting in some strange places, except for my hands and crotch. They were getting numb.

I downed some soup and a sandwich in Fraser and struggled on to Granby. There I entered a drugstore and purchased a small tin of aspirin. I had to ask the clerk to open the container for me.

"It's hard to explain, but my fingers are numb," I said.

I gave out at Hot Sulphur Springs and secured a room in a hotel. It was a long night. I hurt too much to sleep, even with the aspirin. If some great seer had then said to me, "In three years you will ride from Lakewood to Hot Sulphur in *one* day, not a day and a half," I would have retched. That's 107 miles.

The morning ride down Byers Canyon was a delight, but by the time I turned onto Highway 134, six miles north of Kremmling, I was beginning to feel fatigue. Another biker came down off Gore Pass and stopped to talk. My condition must have worried him, because he offered me some lemonade. I should have accepted. He had been on the road for a month and had yet to purchase a meal in a restaurant or stay in a motel. Short on food, he needed directions.

"Your best bet is to go into Kremmling for groceries, even though it is out of your way," I said. "The next towns north are Walden or

Steamboat Springs, and they're pretty far." This is big country.

I was very disappointed that I could not get the bike over Gore Pass without stopping, even though the rear tire no longer rubbed.

"This is the dumbest thing," I repeated.

I was determined this time, however, not to walk the bike. When I did top the pass, I decided to sit down and celebrate by smoking a cigarette. It didn't taste very good.

I envisioned a coast into Toponas. That wasn't the case. There were still lots of hills. A quart of chocolate milk and microwaved burger did not help much as I gazed at a big grade off to the south. Somewhere between McCoy and Bond I approached a local to replenish water. I was told that water was too precious for them to part with their own supply but a spring was farther down the road. I never found the spring.

State Bridge seemed like an oasis. There was what appeared to be a restaurant. Half a dozen ramshackle cottages sat north of the Colorado River near a dirt road which led to Kremmling. With my cottony mouth I inquired about the availability of lodging. The lady proprietor glared at me.

"That would be six dollars—cash," she said.

"Great," I gasped and took out my wallet.

"I suppose you'll be wantin' clean bedding?"

"That would be nice."

She marched into the third cabin, gathered sheets and blankets from the bed, carried the pile out to the porch and gave it a lusty shake. Dust billowed out. Satisfied, she returned the bedding and threw it down on the mattress.

This night there was no sleep. Every muscle in my body screamed. I was sure that this was what it was like to have polio. I was also very dehydrated. I had tried to fix that with beer. There was good Mexican food, but I could not eat much.

South of State Bridge, there is a monster hill separating drainages to the Eagle and Colorado rivers. Why the hill is not called a pass, I will never know. It was a four- or five-mile grunt up the thing after just a glass of O.J. the next morning. I still couldn't eat. The lack of food was beginning to tell. I had to get off the bike and walk some. The far side, once reached, had cattle crossings which I chose to walk over also. I coasted into Wolcott and later bought some lunch in Eagle. I thought Glenwood Canyon would be fun, but I was too busy watching traffic to enjoy it. Twice I saw that trucks were converging on me, so I stopped and moved off the road. There was a strong wind from the west, which made me crank hard even though it was downhill.

I checked in at the Colorado Hotel in Glenwood Springs and called home. My family was worried about me and they were cross because I had not called sooner. I had purposely avoided any communication, because I was afraid I would quit. My gusto was fading.

"I have never punished my body like this," I said. "Tomorrow, I'm gonna throw the bike on a train and come home or, if I feel really good, take it easy with a short ride just to Rifle."

Then I called John Reed who lived in Glenwood Springs and told him what I was doing. "You need some R and R," he said. "I'll be right over to pick you up and we'll have dinner."

I shuddered when I saw that his mode of transportation was a motorcycle, but at least the seat was soft. John fed me beer and hamburgers at his house, took me for a relaxing dip in the hot springs pool, filled me with Jim Beam, and slid me under my hotel room door.

I arrived in Rifle at about 9:30 A.M. and had breakfast. I decided to push onward north toward Meeker. The valley was gorgeous and there was now little traffic. The ride was a lot easier, with gentle grades. I arrived tired, but not suffering from complete exhaustion. I have since learned that, even without adequate preparation, after three days of riding you start to get it together. A new set of hurts was evident, however. Both nipples were abraded from wind flutter of my salt-caked T-shirt. My lips were breaking out with fever blisters from the sun and wind exposure. Sunburn on my arms and legs was the least of my worries. I had quit wearing the jock strap. It was adding new grooves to my bottom. I did my nightly laundry and hung it on my mobile drying rack. I was aghast at what I saw. The rear tire had a big tear and the tube was protruding. If I called home for a rescue now, they would really be mad. Meeker was at the end of the world.

It was Saturday night and shops would soon be closed for the weekend. I found a Western Auto store. They had tires. I pleaded with the owner to help me change them. He was very kind.

"If your fingers are numb, I guess I can do that," he said. "But I don't understand how the chain threads around that thing." He pointed.

"It's called a derailleur. I can deal with that part of it." I had never pulled a wheel from a ten speed in my life.

It's a good crank north over Nine Mile Gap toward Craig. The country is very open and lovely, with little habitation. I ran out of water near Hamilton. At a store there, I was told they had no water.

It was obvious that they wanted to sell me pop. I found a farmer who replenished my water supply, complete with ice.

From Steamboat Springs, I called Anne to tell her I would be in Estes Park in two days. "Don't come yet," she said. "I can't leave that early to drive up to meet you."

Looking for a respite, I spent a day with Luke and Janet Studer at their ranch. It was great to be off the Destroyer. I headed south toward Rabbit Ears Pass after a good night's rest. That hill is a bitch from the west, eight miles of up. I still had a day to kill, so at Muddy Pass I turned east into North Park. At Coalmont, I was pondering what to do about hot sticky asphalt when I heard a shout from behind. I turned in the goo and rode back toward a house.

"Aren't you going to have some ice tea and cookies?" a lady asked. She had fed the Bikecentennial tourers the previous year and just couldn't get out of the habit. Delightful.

From Walden, I had an easy fun ride over Willow Creek Pass and into Grand Lake. While having dinner there, I spotted a tourer riding slowly down the main street with an incredible load. I hurried out to talk. He was from Georgia and had spent the day recovering from the trip over Trail Ridge Road. He had never been on a grind like that. He couldn't make the top by nightfall so he descended the west side with a flashlight in his hand. I was not surprised. On the back of his bike were two huge panniers, tent, sleeping bag, military first-aid kit, a spare wheel with mounted tire, and a carpenter's saw.

The ranger at the gate to Rocky Mountain National Park appraised my bike and me. "This is a very high road you are heading toward, over twelve thousand," he said.

"I know that, I have been over six passes already. I think I'll be all right." My lips were caked with blood and it hurt to talk.

"Suit yourself."

Some people in an RV shouted and waved encouragement as they passed me on a switchback. I felt good, but I knew there was a long haul ahead. Past the Poudre Lakes I "hit the wall." I had absolutely no energy left. I stopped and looked down at the meandering stream far below and up at the endless ribbon of asphalt. I had the makings of a meal in my bag, but had real reservations about choking it down now. Perhaps the dextrose tablets would work. I ate a few and drank the rest of my water. The tablets helped.

There is a visitor's center and museum at the top of "old" Fall River Pass, a one-way gravel road from the east. Sitting next to the museum by a stone wall which broke the wind, I munched on cheese, rolls, and fruit. Tourists walked over to ask if I had ridden "that thing" all the way and how I stayed warm in the chilly atmosphere. I was elated, but I was also worried. More climbing remained.

When I topped out at the Rock Cut, high in the tundra, I was flat dingey. It was probably the lack of oxygen. This was the greatest "high" of my life. I rode like crazy, stealing glances at Arrowhead and Inkwell lakes, where I had backpacked. The views of Longs Peak and Forest Canyon were fantastic. I passed cars creeping along the down-hill grade, their drivers wary of the sharp dropoff to the south. It was a glorious, speedy descent. At Many Parks Curve, a station wagon pulled slowly out into my path.

"Move it or park it," I shouted to passengers staring wide-eyed from the open back window. The car sped away.

Rounding the last turn to Fish Hatchery Road, I glimpsed a huge auto in my tiny mirror. It hung on me and would not pass. I was angry. I had traveled over five hundred miles without serious jeopardy and this guy was going to wipe me out in the last half mile. I stopped the bike, whipped down the kick stand and stormed back to the car to raise hell with the driver. It was my father.

I sat on the cabin front porch, beer in hand, reviewing the trip with Anne and my dad. My thighs burned, both skin and muscles. My rear was raw. Hands, upper back, and crotch were numb. Lips and chest were scabbed. I could not stop talking. I felt just great, and my mind was racing. The seed had been planted for a whole set of challenging adventures.

My thoughts about the Destroyer have now come full circle. First ignorance, then despair. Later disdain, as I learned to appraise a bike by looking for brazed lugs and simply hefting it. The Destroyer waits patiently in Estes Park. Like all of us, it occasionally needs some strokes. Now and then I gratefully comply, for the heavy old thing probably saved my life.

CHAPTER 2

THE BOULDER CRAZIES

I was unsure of Anne's reaction to a pitch for more toys. I elected to pull all the stops and appeal to her sympathy.

"Wife, I need a new bike," I said. "The guys in Boulder have asked me to join them for a little tour. Compared to me, they are kids. I'm ten years older than any of them. It will be tough enough to get ready on some new iron. On the Destroyer I would die." I paused. Had I whined too much?

"So get a new bike," she said.

The people at Life Cycle were very helpful and they didn't bad mouth my old machine. They must have realized that I had an emotional attachment to that heavy old thing. When they determined my price range, a Motobecane Super Mirage was pulled from the rack. It was a ten-speed black touring bike with cast vinyl covers on the handlebars. The bike had stem-mounted shifters and brake lever extensions like my old bike. I knew that cool dudes don't condone these devices, but I was used to them. The bike was not a super lightweight, but it was twelve pounds less than what I had been pedaling. I bought it.

That was the easy part. Then I had to get myself ready. A year had passed since my sojourn onto the mountain highways and I was again out of shape. On three successive days I went for a ride into the foothills. Each day I made it a little tougher and longer. The last day I rode about forty miles.

"I may have done it to myself," I reported to Anne. "My rear is really sore. I may not be able to ride at all tomorrow." It was another episode of too much too quickly.

The guys picked me up and we drove west. We had intended to ride north out of Wolcott, but it was raining hard there. We drove on to Rifle, where it was dry, and mouted our bikes. It was a pleasant ride over familiar terrain. I need not have worried about my bike or my body. Compared to my new Motobecane, their bicycles were junk. My warm-up rides had built some speed and endurance. At least no one blasted out ahead of me. Best of all, my fanny was O.K.

We spent the first night at Meeker in a motel. The second night we stayed in a condominium south of Steamboat Springs. Everyone leaped into the swimming pool in their riding shorts. I grinned the next morning when I heard shouts from the others as they dressed. The chamois liners in their pants had not dried. I didn't have any clothing this fancy. My shorts were dry, but no one knew that. Someone asked me at breakfast, "Well, numb nuts, are your freezing pants going to make you ride like a tiger today?"

"I'll be fierce," I said.

No one was fierce by the time we reached Yampa. We were bucking a ferocious head wind. The road was dead flat and I had only two gears left. It wasn't fun any more, so we quit and loaded the bikes on the van. South of Toponas, I said, "This is a good hill. Does anyone want to ride down?"

We flipped to see who would drive, unloaded, and raced down the slope. I stopped at the bottom and turned to watch Jim Bodin hurtling around the last turn. He pulled up to me. "That was some ride," he said.

"Do you ever think about what it would do to your body if you fell at that speed?" I asked.

"I try not to think about it. That would be Hurt City."

Fifteen years later, Larry McLaughlin, an experienced triathlete from Utah cycling in the "Ride The Rockies" tour would crash less than ten miles south of there, at State Bridge. He would be grievously injured after failing to negotiate a similar downhill right turn onto the concrete bridge deck.

My first junket with the Boulder group was rather modest. The pack increased in size yearly as more people opted to go. I did not ride every year, but I was along for five tours in Colorado and two in New Mexico. The first had five bikers in one vehicle. The most recent had thirty-two riders and five vans.

The ride was usually held in May. It was luxury touring, with a sag wagon stocked with amenities: food, water, beer, parts, pumps, and patches. All of our luggage was transported. No one was saddled with the continual chore of driving; we took turns. The first driver would park the vehicle (usually a rented VW van) six miles down the road, get his bike out, lock up, hide the key in a prearranged location, hop on his bike and take off. The number two driver would take over from there and so on. If someone got pooped, they could just stay with the van. It worked pretty well, but my business partner Arch drove very little. The van never caught up with him.

At night we would settle into a motel, hotel, or condo for a shower, toddies, and a gourmet dinner. Breakfast was leisurely, with each rider on the road at the hour of his choice. Arch and I would usually start early—he because he wanted to be first to finish, I because I didn't want to be last.

The route was always selected by our leader, Woody. He had a curious ability to select great rides without actually having ridden them in a car or on a bike. He would consult with others on occasion, but we usually had no knowledge about where the yearly excursion would take us until we received a letter in the spring. In recent years, the mailing has contained a liability waiver for our signature. I can't blame Woody for this. The lawsuit abuse by our society is out of control.

The group consisted of businessmen. Many were involved in real estate, sometimes competing against each other. Woody had retired from the dental profession to manage real estate holdings. Arch retired from an engineering business which he and I partly owned. All of our touring people were very compatible, even though we had three distinct types of bikers. We always had a few hard-core gunners, very serious riders who rode as if it were a race. Then there was the middle group, guys like me, who rode moderately hard but it was no disgrace to take time out for a beer or lie down in the shade. The third type consisted of our "flower children," those who preferred to sit in their own van smoking pot and listening to the stereo. If they rode a bike ten miles, that would for them be a really big day of cycling.

As years passed, the latter group disappeared. It's kind of a shame. They were fun. Those of us who were more straight arrow did not approve of their illegal activity; neither did we ostracize them because of it. The pot smokers just chose a different and infrequent avenue for relief from worldly stress. It was the times.

I always had the gnawing fear that we might be arrested—guilt by association and all that. We stopped to rest outside the entrance to the New Mexico State Prison one year. That made me nervous. Our vans had a variety of aromas. A guard walked out to investigate, shook his head in disbelief, and strolled away.

None of us older folks were exactly Puritans. One year we started from Glenwood Springs in early afternoon and cranked south toward Redstone. For a while I rode along with Bob Mistler, an attorney. He was trying not to think about cigarettes, the normal kind, because he had quit smoking to make the ride easier. It wasn't working. I had vowed to do the same and was having a similar problem. "How long have you been off the weeds?" he asked. I looked at my watch and gave him a report accurate to the minute.

We reached the Redstone Lodge, showered, and headed for the bar. It started to snow. By early evening it was obvious that we were in for a heavy storm. The morning ride looked to be in serious jeopardy. Bob and I decided to make the best of the situation, relax, and party it up.

"Let's have another drink. It's my turn to buy," he said. "Here, have a smoke." I lit up the offered cigarette and dealt the cards.

In the morning I was badly hung over. Groping my way to the window, I looked out. Snow covered the tree limbs and forest floor, but the paved driveway in front of our building was free of flakes. It was only damp. We would be riding and I felt like the very devil.

I struggled up McClure Pass, which seemed inordinately steep. Many riders passed me. It took some time for the cold air to clear my head. There were two deer at the road edge near the top. They stared at me and I said, "Don't ever do this." They bounded into the trees.

The downslope to Hotchkiss is crossed occasionally by railroad tracks at a very acute angle. Some of our people neglected to slow down and turn hard in order to align properly for a crossing perpendicular to the steel. Their tires dropped into the groove by a rail and they could not recover. It was the dope smokers who crashed and burned. Their "Mary Jane" was at once the cause and the cure. Perception of the rider may have been faulty but he really didn't care. I was driving our van during these episodes and had cause to double back to search for wounded riders. I was the only one with a first-aid kit, of sorts. There was a fair amount of road rash and torn clothing, but no serious injuries.

On occasion the flower van would miss a turn and get lost or one of their riders would forget to pick up his bike and put it in the vehicle.

"What's happenin', man?"

"I just can't find my bike."

"Did you have it when we left Boulder?"

On one trip, we rode over Hoosier Pass into Fairplay for a night at the hotel. For dinner, a long single table was set for our group. I could not understand why so many riders would sit down to eat and then disappear. I was talking across the table to Arch and then I wasn't. He was gone. I found him rolling on the bed in our room having a dialogue with the wallpaper. He and others had partaken of some exotic mushrooms during the cocktail hour. They were hallucinogenic. I went to find our best substitute for a doctor. That would be Woody, the ex-dentist. He wasn't much help.

I left the group after one day of cycling together and rode alone into Lakewood. It was mostly downhill. Kenosha Pass is quick from the west. Crow Hill, north of Bailey, was long and mean. It was a Saturday and I had made a commitment to sing with a church choir in Central City the next morning. I decided to ride my bike to that event. The ride into the mountains along Clear Creek has a nice gentle gradient, but above Black Hawk the road steepens severely. I was sweating heavily when I arrived at the church. I wondered if the choir robe would shield me from offending my neighbor vocalists. Stinky bikers should sit in their own pew.

In May of 1985, the Boulder Crazies annual "gut grinder" consisted of a second venture into New Mexico. It was a strenuous four-day trip. The first day we rode from Antonito, Colorado, to Chama, New Mexico, over La Manga and Cumbres passes. Day two took us to Taos via Tierra Amarilla, Tres Piedras, and the striking bridge spanning the gorge of the Rio Grande River. On the third day we journeyed south into testing hills before lunch at Mora and then north toward Angel Fire. The paving on our winding road through a broad valley gave out in mid-afternoon. We loaded our bikes onto the rack of our van and settled in for a respite while our driver guided the vehicle through a cavern of trees up into the mountains on two ruts for a roadway. We were not talkative, listening to classical music on the tape deck. I tried to avoid spilling beer on myself as the van jostled us back and forth on the seats. I was contemplating the climb over Red River Pass on the morrow. Suddenly we emerged from half light into a palette of color, wild mountain flowers glowing in the sunlight and wafting in the breeze. The blossoms stretched before us, flooding an entire meadow with pastel hues. We scrambled out of the vehicle with our cameras to take pictures of the flowers and each other. Our driver adjusted the music to maximum volume. Vivaldi thundered into the hills. It was a glorious moment, replete with a lift for the senses and a spirit of comraderie. We had endured a hard physical challenge together and been richly rewarded. It turned out that our photos did not do the experience justice. It had to be implanted in your memory.

That was the good part about these rides. The bad part was that I would come to find them too easy. Oh, the physical trial was always present—either hills, distance, or speed. I am not a racer. The group today is so macho that I can hardly keep up, so I don't try. They form packs of four or five and speed down the road in line, pulling and changing the lead as if they were in the Tour de France. I just truck along, usually by myself, looking at the scenery and thinking great thoughts. The others talk basic gear head and I can't even pronounce the brand names of their bikes.

But the mental test is lacking. It is credit card touring with a sag wagon, expensive, mostly problem-free. Because of the planning by Woody, little head work is required. In that respect, it is not unlike some tours managed by commercial operators, who guide their charges from inn to inn for a pampered eatathon. There is never much doubt about where you will be spending the night or whether you will arrive there safely and in comfort. Your luggage will disappear for the day and magically reappear in the evening. The Crazies would not dream of strapping panniers to their classy featherweight machines.

After my most recent trip with them, we lounged in the van riding back to our homes. Someone asked to look at my journal. I handed him the little red book and he glanced through it quickly.

"Bob, I'd like to go with you on one of your trips without support," he said. "It sounds challenging."

"It is, but I'm not sure that you would enjoy it. It's a different scene with all the weight. You bike like someone driving a Porsche. I drive a truck. Call me some time and we'll arrange a trip." I was pretty sure that I would never hear from him. They just don't like to travel loaded.

CHAPTER 3

MONTANA

Montana didn't concern me. I was afraid of Wyoming. I would lie awake at night planning the trip north and west and I would worry about the huge yawning expanse of the state next to Colorado. I worried about the wind and the long stretches of highway with no habitation. I worried about snakes and heat. I worried about riding an interstate, which I had never done. But mostly, I worried about boredom.

In 1979, my oldest son, Bruce, lived in Whitefish, Montana. It seemed like a good idea to visit him by bicycle. Anne could drive up and retrieve me. We had a house guest from Germany who wanted to see the West. He and two of my daughters, Lisa and Nancy, could accompany Anne in the car. It would be a lark for everyone.

I had some new bicycle goodies which I wanted to test. My engineering company did structural consulting, mostly for architectural firms. If one of our clients was contemplating an addition to his personal residence, we usually did the design gratis. We figured it was good P.R. Jim Bershof, an architect in Denver, was going to add some space to his house, so I worked on the structural design personally and our mailed statement for services rendered said "No Charge." Jim is an avid biker who often rides his bike to work. I used to go in his office, heft his bike, and lust after it.

Jim thoughtfully gave me a one-hundred-dollar gift certificate at Life Cycle, which he knew I frequented. "I was going to buy you some exotic parts," he said, "but I thought you ought to make the choice." He did the right thing. At that time, I thought Campy was a baseball catcher.

I presented the certificate in exchange for a tire pump, a back rack, two panniers, and some tan touring shorts. The clerk gave me good advice on the panniers, which were "seconds" and thus affordable. "Don't get something ultra large or you will kill yourself lugging everything you own," he said. I opted for medium size bags with one exterior pocket on each.

On the first day out from Lakewood, I went over Loveland Pass to Silverthorne. I was a mess when I arrived. You can't hang your buns on a drafting stool all year and stay in exquisite condition. My training regimen was to work it out on the road, which I don't recommend. I suffered from exhaustion, dehydration, and muscle soreness. The worst part was that I could not eat enough to maintain any strength until I had ridden for a few days. Then I could eat anything in sight.

I wasn't particularly hungry when I woke up and the restaurants were not open. I was nervous and anxious to get on the road. So I mounted the bike and rode thirty-eight miles to Kremmling for breakfast. This is something which I came to do a lot—ride before I ate. It must be my Type A personality pushing me to get at the job at hand. I have known athletes who threw up before they went into a game. I was not that bad, but I was very antsy to get on the road.

The trip north is a super bicycle ride. Along the Blue River, it is mostly a gentle downgrade through a lovely valley with the Eagle's Nest Wilderness Area on the left. You cross the Colorado River just south of Kremmling and follow Muddy Creek up a wide valley which narrows into the forests. It is a delight. I crossed Rabbit Ears Pass and rode into Steamboat Springs for the night. That day I had met two other bikers.

Traveling west on U.S. 40 the next day, I arrived in Craig before noon. I stopped at a convenience store north of town and lifted my bike up onto a sidewalk by grasping the handlebars and seat. I don't do that any more. The bike was so heavy that the leather seat popped off its metal frame and I could not force it back on. I rode back in to Craig, standing up, to look for a bike shop. It took a great deal of effort for a pro to get my saddle remounted. I had wasted two hours.

Once again on the road, I made a long sweeping curve to the left into sage brush country to the north. Grouse exploded out of the borrow pits adjacent and startled me. There was virtually no traffic. I was alone in huge country. It was a little unsettling, but an awesome experience. I really had nothing to be concerned about. Just keep plugging along and eventually you will get to Baggs, I told myself.

I stayed in a hotel which I later discovered had been used by Robert Leroy Parker and Harry Longabaugh—Butch Cassidy and the Sundance Kid. I understand that it was destroyed by fire after my visit. I showered in a quaint arrangement of pipes and porcelain, changed clothing, and went to a bar nearby. It was crowded with an incompatible assortment of cowboys from the ranches and roughnecks from the drilling rigs. I was wearing a dark blue jogging suit with lime green and white racing stripes. My outfit did not fit into the decor very well. When a fight started at the back of the room, I eased quietly out the front door.

I gingerly lifted my rump onto a stool in a second spirits emporium while a hard-looking character next to me ran his eyes slowly up and down my snappy outfit. He didn't say anything. "I just biked in from Denver," I volunteered. He still didn't say anything, for about five minutes.

"Do you mean on a pedal bike?" he asked. I nodded yes. "Holy shit. Hey guys, listen to this." Instantly, several cans of beer appeared before me on the bar and I had admirers probing me with questions. It was all I could do to get out of there gracefully without soaking up all the suds in southern Wyoming.

I retreated to the only restaurant I could find, which was about to close. They brought me a very basic meal of roast pork, mashed potatoes and gravy, and green beans. It was abundant and deliciously fatfree. When I awakened before dawn the next morning, I decided to ride immediately in semi-darkness even though I knew it was fifty miles to the next bit of civilization, on Interstate 80. A big buck leaped out of some willows as I left town.

I settled in for the long flat ride north, playing games guessing at the distance to prominent bluffs and ravines. Jackrabbits, ground hogs, and grouse were everywhere. Antelope stared at me and I gave them various salutations. I love to talk to the animals.

I gobbled sausage and pancakes in a diner at Creston and turned west on the shoulder of I-80. Several of the western states allow bicycle travel on the interstate highways. Wyoming is one of them. I consider an interstate to be the safest place for a cyclist, except in and near urban areas, where entry and exit ramps are very hazardous. If the shoulder is smooth and free of debris, a biker has his own highway. However, the noise is pretty bad.

Some motorcyclists and I left the highway to hide under a bridge during a rain shower. We had a good talk. I have found all motorcycle riders, even the black leather jacket wearers, to be very friendly, but you have to talk to them first. Some are intimidated by bicyclists, believe it or not. They know you enjoy some parallel aspects of their sport, but they seem embarrassed because their physical effort is nil.

There were no unusual happenings until I approached Rock Springs. A full can of beer came spinning at me from a pickup, spraying liquid on my body. The can did not hit me or the bike. A driver in a car behind the culprit shook his head in sympathy as he passed. I found a beat-up hotel in town, but when they took me to my room, there were still people in it. I left. I signed in for a room at a motel, but it was a black hole and the air conditioner did not work. I left there also, getting a little discouraged. I finally found lodging on the west side of town. The price was ridiculous. Rock Springs made a very poor impression on me. My patience was wearing thin and I was very tired. I had ridden over 130 miles that day.

About ten miles north of Rock Springs, U.S. 191 climbs onto a huge plateau. The paving there was awful and it drove me batty. Cracks in the asphalt were pounding me into oblivion. I was afraid that spokes would break and considered heading back. A study of the map on my handlebar bag revealed that the alternatives were not good, so I pressed on. The hammering finally quit (bad stuff always does get better) and I saw the town of Eden ahead, its garden of trees the only green for miles. I bought a can of pop and kept cranking northward, conversing all the while with myself and the antelope. I could see the mountains of the Bridger-Teton National Forest far ahead on my right. I had been totally wrong about fearing Wyoming. I enjoyed the solitude and the vastness. It wasn't boring at all. It was great.

Boulder, Wyoming, received me twice. I stopped at a service station for refreshment and blasted north. There was a dark mass in the sky ahead of me and it was closing fast. I thought it was rain. Wrong! Loud raps on my helmet and sharp stings to my arms and shoulders forced me into a quick one-eighty. I raced back to Boulder and hid from hail under the service station canopy.

The plan had been for Anne to follow me. Not each day, mile by mile. That is a drag for both biker and driver. I was to keep her informed about my location and she would meet me somewhere on the road for one night. This could be very supportive when I was strung out in unfamiliar country. I called her from the motel, which I considered to be little short of the Taj Mahal. On the nightstand, I had peanuts and a glass of beer. "I am a long way out from Denver," I said. "You will have to leave very early to catch me in one day."

"Where are you?"

"Pinedale, Wyoming. I'll go north from here on 191, but I won't go into Jackson. Have you got the map handy?"

"O.K. I see where you are. Where will you go, then?"

"I'll head into Idaho on 89 and then 26."

"How early do you think we should leave?"

"I would try for 3 A.M. No later than 4." Wasn't I a sweetie?

I did have breakfast in Pinedale before getting on the bike. It was a chilly morning. I crossed the Green River and contemplated the increase in grade ahead. It looked like it was time to strip down to my climbing attire. I pulled off into a parking area and was removing my long pants when a highway patrolman shot by and gave me a careful look. My change to shorts and T-shirt turned out to be premature, because in no time at all I was over "The Rim" heading downward on one of the best rides of my life. I could see clouds *below* me to the west, hanging in pretty valleys. I bombed down the highway, fingers numbing and teeth chattering. I did not realize how lucky I was to have a full belly and have burned little energy so far that day. I would learn about that later.

The road drops down, down, down through wooded slopes into a lovely valley containing the Hoback River. The Hoback drains into the Snake, which I followed to Alpine Junction. There, I could see a big storm building to the south. It looked like it was heading my way, so I decided to run for it. This might have worked if the road around Palisades Reservoir had been level and straight. It was neither. I got wet but I kept on riding. West of Swan Valley I started to worry about my family. Where were they? Was it possible for them to miss me? I had stayed visible to the highway all day when I stopped to eat or rest. I would be coming up on Idaho Falls soon, where I could get lost and they would never find me. What if they have car trouble? Should we have agreed on a rendezvous point or communication hub in case of a screw-up? I was sweating heavily, riding without a shirt, and drinking tons of water. I think I was cooking on nervous energy, pushing up to my limits because it didn't seem right for my family to find me standing at the side of the road. It had been an outstanding day's ride and I wanted to reel in as many miles as I could.

They passed me one-quarter of a mile east of Ririe, Idaho. They shouted, "Daddy, Daddy," like they always do even though they are no longer little kids. Boy, it was good to see them. We all talked and laughed at a service station where Anne pulled in to park. Lisa rode my bike around the pumps to see what a loaded tourer was like. They were very tired. They had stopped only to gas up and purchase take-out food. I was very tired also, and kind of hyper. They drove ahead to Rigby to find a motel and I followed. That was twelve more miles. I had already covered 144.

Everyone, including the waitress, was incredulous at how much I ate for dinner. I was like a rampaging vacuum cleaner, sucking up everything on my plate and theirs. The lad from Germany, Rene, was amazed at the size of our West. He had never sat in a car for such a long period or even imagined such gigantic country. We had a great evening, but I did not relish their leaving me behind the next day.

Two blocks down the street the following morning, I threw my chain. I walked back to the motel to free and align it, so that I could clean the grease off my hands when I was done. Everyone but Anne was still asleep. I started again and soon found a market in Roberts, where I stocked up on groceries. Then things started to deteriorate. A sign on the ramp to I-15 prohibited my entry. I only needed eight miles on the freeway. I asked around and was told I could go north on another road, only it was not paved. I nursed the bike over dirt and gravel up to Highway 33. Then I headed west and it got hot. From Mud Lake the road stretched northwest in a sizzling strip of asphalt which disappeared in heat waves far up on the horizon. I consumed great quantities of water and stopped to dunk my head in the only visible irrigation ditch. I struggled towards Blue Dome, which appeared on my map as Mecca. Blue Dome turned out to be nothing. No town. Nothing. I asked at a farmhouse for water and filled my two bottles at a garden hose.

Most tourers carry two or three water bottles in cages attached to the bike frame. I did not, at that time. I had one standard bottle outside. It held something over a half liter. In one of my panniers, hopefully on the shady side, I carried a large anodized aluminum bottle which held over a liter. I rolled it carefully in my fancy long pants, to keep the water cool and my trousers pressed. It also gave me an excuse to stop. I would fiddle with bottles and rest. I don't even now carry a full load of water unless the terrain is uninhabited. The added weight is very noticeable. I drank all I could and ate something. I was depressed because my family had somehow missed me. I found out later that they had unknowingly passed me—they on the interstate, me on the dirt.

This was a long, though gentle, climb to Gilmore Divide. I was traveling slowly so the sweat did not evaporate quickly and I was soaked.

I could tell that I was in trouble in arid territory, so I started to ration my remaining water by mileage markers. Two quarts of liquid does not last long on a hot ride. There were no houses in sight. From time to time I thought I saw rain clouds over the Lemhi Range to my left. Then I realized they were smoke.

It was a relief to top that long upgrade. I still had considerable miles ahead to Leadore, but on a downslope the water situation did not seem so critical. I sucked the last of the liquid from my exterior bottle and pressed on. I was too tired and dehydrated to travel effectively. An upslope wind was impeding my motion and repeating stretches of loose gravel were a threat. Fur seemed to grow in my mouth and I knew that even if water had been available it was too late to put my system in balance for that day. I would have to rehydrate overnight.

As I pedaled weakly into Leadore, I glanced to my left and saw that the only motel was closed. I parked the bike outside a bar, hurried in and sloshed down two draft beers instantly. The bartender told me that I might camp in the City Park. I rolled the bike over to a cafe, went inside and ordered their ham dinner.

As always, I sat facing toward a window where the view of my machine's handlebars and saddle projecting above the sill could give me solace. I attacked the meal, huge slabs of ham one-half inch thick, french fries, rolls, salad, and iced tea. A young man outside stopped in his tracks to gaze at my bike. He moved closer and bent over to study the components. Then he straightened, reached down to grab the stem and saddle, and lifted my bicycle.

I was across the room and out the door like a missile. The fellow turned toward me, still holding the bike, his eyes wide and mouth open. "I wasn't gonna take it," he said.

"I know that," I said. I smiled and the valleys in his forehead softened a bit. "It's just that when you lift it that way, the seat sometimes pops off. Then I am in a pickle." He was lowering the bike.

"Oh. It does seem heavy."

"It's not so bad now. My water bottles are empty. They're inside the cafe."

"How far have you come?"

"From Denver."

"Lordy, that's a long way. Where are you headed?"

"Whitefish, Montana."

"That's a ways, too."

"But I'm well over half way there."

"Yep. Where you stayin'? The motel's shut down."

"In your park, I guess."

"Do you have a tent? There's cattle in there."

"No, just a sleeping bag. I think I'll be O.K."

"I suppose. Good luck."

I finished my meal, which included a giant dish of ice cream—all for five bucks. Then I filled my water bottles, bought two cans of Oly, and pedaled toward my campsite. It was a wooded patch west of the town. I leaned my bike against a tree and threw down my poncho as a ground cloth. Then, with displeasure, I inserted my salt-caked grimy body into the sleeping bag. I opened a can of beer. I could hear cattle trampling around but hoped they would avoid me in the moonlight. The grass was soft and I was dead tired. It was difficult to stay awake to drink the beer.

I was up and on the road early the next morning, without washing or breakfast. Ducks burst out of ponds adjacent as I sped down the highway. I approached them with little noise, but the birds could not tolerate the intrusion of a human with whirling devices just above their sanctuary. It was almost fifty miles to Salmon, where I devoured a tasty omelette brunch. I hoped that I did not offend anyone in the restaurant. I was unkempt and I must have smelled like Tarzan. At least I could wash up a little in their restroom. I pushed on north and saw that the amount of smoke in the air was increasing. There had to be great forest fires burning west of me. I went through North Fork and passed a bunch of guys who looked a lot worse off than I, even at a distance. They were fire fighters resting near their trucks and tents. They waved. I waved back but I was too intent on the hill ahead to stop. I later regretted that many times. It would have been neat to talk to them.

The road got steeper and I was pestered by a huge horsefly. It flew around my head, arms, and shoulders. I could not generate enough speed to leave it behind. I must have been really rank. Sweat was dripping out of my helmet in little rivulets so I took off the brain bucket and fastened it over my front bag. Then the fly had a field day. I flailed at that creature most of the way up Lost Trail Pass. He did take my mind off the climb.

At the top, I leaned my bike against a sign and sat down to recuperate with some nourishment. A tiny lady came over the pass from the north on a small bike almost hidden by all her worldly possessions. She came over to visit.

"Hi," I said. "Where are you from?"

"Seattle. I'm going to Jacksonville."

"That will take some time." I tried not to stare. She looked to be in very good condition. She wasn't panting and sweating like I had been. Her mouth was in bad shape, however, like mine. She had severely blistered lips. I thought girls used lipstick to prevent this sort of thing. I just plain forget to apply lip balm.

"It's no problem," she said. "I have a month and it won't take that long. I can do 150 miles a day." I did not doubt that she could.

"Do you need some food? I'd be glad to share," I said.

"No thanks." She was gone.

I spent the night in Darby. It was bliss to take a hot shower. I peered at my map and added numbers, "One hundred nineteen miles today," I said. I wasn't keeping up with the gal from Washington. "Oh well, what the hell." It's tough to grow old.

It took the better part of two more days to reach Whitefish. My elbows were starting to hurt, which I blamed on the Montana roads. They were not the best. They appeared to be maintained by crews with tar buckets and teaspoons. I rode around the west side of Flathead Lake because my map showed it to be the scenic route. It was, but it was also a hilly tiring ride and I was becoming anxious to see folks. Pumped up with adrenaline, I charged the last five miles into Whitefish only to discover Bruce's house empty of people. I bought a six-pack of beer and stretched out on the grass.

After a few days with Bruce, we put Lisa on a train to Washington and we put my bike on a rack on the back of our Saab. On the drive back to Denver I made excuses to retrace parts of my route so I could show off and describe every rut and point out where I had peed. "This is a tougher hill than it looks," I would say.

"I'm sure that it is," Anne would reply kindly. Nancy and Rene were bored. It did not occur to me to take a different route, just to stimulate everyone's interest. I drove on relentlessly toward Pinedale so we could stay in the same motel which I had enjoyed.

"You will love it," I said. "It is really quite nice." We checked in and went to our rooms. Anne looked around and then she laughed and looked at me.

"Are you really serious?" she asked. "Is this your idea of a comfort castle?" I paused and looked around too. She was right. The room was a model of austerity. On a bike trip you see some things differently.

CHAPTER 4

THE CANNON

Friends ask me what I think about while I am on a long bicycle tour. They probably have the conception that it is very boring chugging along mile after mile with no companionship. It isn't at all that way.

I think about a lot of things, but I do not think about work. As an engineer I have been accustomed to occasional flashes of creative insight which might explode in my head at a strange time, say sitting on the throne or lying in bed. My conscious and subconscious mind will not consider office problems while on a bike tour. I might think about my family and what they are doing, but that occurs mostly at night when I am off the bike. Mostly I am in harmony with my surroundings, studying the land and enjoying it, wondering how it is going to affect me that particular day. I can see, but not always understand, how the land has affected other people, how they set their goals, erected their homes, built their fences, carved their roadways, organized or failed to organize their cities. I want the land to treat me gently, so I spend a copious amount of time planning, anticipating, checking, and changing while I am on a tour. My ultimate destination is always in mind but the tactics for a given day may push me toward an unanticipated location. That's part of the fun.

For instance, my mind dwells a great deal on a very simple chemical compound—water. I have to keep water running through my body, visibly or not, or the worn machine will grind to a halt. I try to avoid water spilling out of the sky or it can ruin my little parade. It is helpful to observe which direction water is running on the earth beside me. When huge quantities of the stuff are flowing in my path, I have to know how and where to cross over. This may be easier said than done. You do not ride a bike across the Columbia, the Mississippi, the Hudson just any old place. A bridge which accepts cars may not accept you. I would like to have some water available at day's end, preferably heated, to cleanse my soiled apparel and body. I would like to have some, preferably frozen, to temper my libation.

I do not want to convey that I am continually in a nervous state of concern about my well being, but a solid conscientious bicycle tourer spends much effort just keeping out of mischief. In the worst-case scenario, my troubles would not be passed on too heavily to my family, because I had a bundle of life insurance provided by my dollars and those of my company. For something less severe, I had major medical coverage. These protective devices, conceived by man, had built-in flaws inherited from their creators, but they soothed me a bit. I knew that sometimes things go completely wrong, as with the Cannon.

There was a time when I took some flak about hunting big game with a .30-.30. "Bob, do the bullets come out end over end?" or "Do you jamb the stock into the ground and shoot it like a mortar?"

Usually I just grinned back at my critics. I knew the classic answers to their barbs and I had a few responses of my own. But I was somewhat envious of their modern scope-sighted rifles. My Model 94 Winchester was starting to look a bit ratty. The wood was chipped and had lost its luster. There was no longer any bluing around the receiver where I grasped the rifle for toting. Maybe it was time for graduation to a huge studly cannon.

I found the perfect rifle for my needs in a dealer's ad in the newspaper. It was a sporterized NATO .30-06 with a Mauser action. Even with a scope, it was affordable. It looked sleek and powerful and was not inordinately heavy. I proudly brought my purchase home and showed it to family members, most of whom yawned.

The rifle needed to be "sighted in," I was informed. I took it to the nearest range, adjacent to the local county landfill. After several punishing shots, my sore shoulder told me to accept the accuracy of scope and rifle. Every time I pulled the bolt, however, the ejecting shell case just lay there in the breech. It didn't fly out to the right. This disturbed me.

I took the rifle back to the dealer. Their man examined it after listening to my story. "This is a defective bolt," he announced. "There is a lug missing which is supposed to eject the cartridge."

"Can you replace the bolt?" I asked.

"We'll replace the whole rifle," he said. I was delighted. It turned out that I never had an opportunity to sight in the replacement rifle that fall. I missed the entire hunting season that year, the .30-06 standing in the corner of my closet. I had no idea that I was storing a time bomb.

The following year, I returned to the county dump with Stan Thorfinnson, who also wanted to check out his rifle. I still was not used to the noise or the hammering I was taking.

"Stan, I think I'm beginning to flinch just in anticipation of the recoil."

"I can see that," he responded. "Why don't you try wearing my new jacket? It has some padding in the shoulder." I donned his coat and leaned out on the bench rest.

I fired fourteen rounds. On the fifteenth the rifle blew apart. There was a strange rasping explosion which the rangemaster quickly identified as a problem. "Cease firing," he shouted.

I looked down at shattered wood and metal. I saw blood all over the end of Stan's jacket sleeve, then on my left hand. It took me a moment to comprehend that I was injured. When the realization took place, I sprinted up an incline to a shack at the end of the firing line. All activity had ceased and gunners were turning to stare at me. I asked for a first-aid kit. There was none. I ran back toward Stan. A thoughtful person donated a clean starched handkerchief to wrap my wound. Stan volunteered to drive me to a hospital. Neither the pain nor the bleeding were intense, but I was afraid to look at my hand. I was very concerned about the blood on Stan's brand new coat.

I was admitted at the emergency room of Saint Anthony Hospital. They asked if I preferred a specific doctor. I told them who to call. I was sure that I needed a good orthopedic surgeon and he was one of the best. We had suffered through an encounter before. Although the good doctor at times displayed the bedside manner of King Kong, I had learned to appreciate his candid talk. If terse is the order of the day, I am no slouch myself.

They loaded me onto a gurney with my left arm and hand supported on a table. A nurse examined the wound until she saw me doing the same and my reaction to it. It looked like a tiny bomb had gone off under the surface behind my thumb. She covered it again.

When the doctor arrived, he walked directly to the table supporting my arm and lifted the draped cloth.

"Wow, you sure have done it to yourself. How did this happen?" He replaced the drape and I explained as he went to a sink to scrub.

"Were you shooting reloads?" he asked.

"No. It was all factory ammo." He returned to lift the cloth and stare at my hand again.

"This sure is a mess. I can see some bone chips, too."

"Look, doctor, you're not helping my morale one bit. Will you be able to save any of my hand?"

"We'll save it all," he replied. He motioned to a nurse who zapped me with a syringe full of goodies and they went to work.

The doctor left orders for me to stay overnight at the hospital for observation. In the morning, I received a telephone call from a client. He is an architect and I was his structural consultant. He was distressed because I had been admitted as a "gun shot wound." My client had visions of some irate, jealous husband blowing me apart and he made the fitting ribald comments.

"Which hand is it?" he asked after I explained the true circumstances.

"Left."

"It's good that it wasn't your drawing hand. You'll be able to get my job out on schedule."

"Thanks for your concern," I said, but I was annoyed with him.

In days to follow, this gentleman, along with one or two others, would comment about how I had the rifle manufacturer, the dealer, and their insurance companies right where I wanted them. Now was my chance to "get well," they said. This was before the giant problems with professional liability claims, but product liability was receiving huge press. I wondered how my client would treat me if I screwed up something on one of his projects. This was the beginning of the end for a lengthy architect-engineer relationship.

I took the remains of the rifle to a gunsmith. He pointed out where bluing had run into a fault near the rear of the exploded barrel. I also took the parts back to the dealer for examination. Their man took my name and said I would hear from them. "You're lucky the bolt held," he added. I hadn't thought about that.

About a week later, I visited the doctor's office. He tenderly removed the dressing. The wound looked bad to me, ugly with sutures and dried blood. The doctor was ecstatic. He called in his partner to show off the results of his handiwork. I felt nauseous, but managed to hang on.

An insurance adjuster called on me. He was very courteous and businesslike. He said they were prepared to make amends for my problems, since the rifle was obviously defective.

"We also want to reimburse you for pain and suffering," he said. "We want to handle this thing for good and don't want you to come at us later with an added claim for your hurts."

"I'm not sure that I can fairly evaluate pain and suffering," I said. "I know that it scared the hell out of me." We stared at each other in silence for about twenty seconds, which is a lengthy void in a verbal exchange.

"How does one hundred dollars sound?" I asked.

"That sounds just fine. Don't misunderstand. I have another case right now with a lady who slipped on a sidewalk. She is hurt less than you and she wants the world. We'll fight her tooth and nail. By the way, do you want another rifle?"

"I think I'll pass."

I believe the check I received was for about eight hundred dollars. That paid for the rifle, doctor bill, hospital bill, a day lost from work, a wasted hunting license, and the pain and suffering. I took part of the money and bought a Browning twenty-gauge superposed shotgun. Today it's worth at least four times what I paid for it. My old Model 94 probably isn't worth a whole lot but I'm very happy with it. I have full strength and mobility in my left hand. Parts are a little numb, but the scars are barely visible.

Some years after the accident, I was hunting elk in the Flat Tops southwest of Deep Lake. I had laid my rifle on the hood of Al Yorke's Bronco. It was the second day of the season and an entourage of his friends drove up to commiserate about their lack of luck. I heard a guffaw.

"This is rich. Who in the hell thinks he's gonna kill an elk with a .30-.30?" I didn't know what to say but Al did.

"That rifle belongs to Bob, here. He got his elk yesterday. It took one shot."

I could have hugged him.

CHAPTER 5

RISK AND FEAR

I know sportsmen who won't hunt elk in some of the most prolific areas of southern Colorado. They are afraid they will be shot by a Texan. I'm serious. I wonder if they ever considered that their own rifle could blow up.

What makes you tense? Is it, "This is your captain speaking . . ."? You are better off riding with him than in your car, in spite of the amount of debris falling from the sky these days. If you have so far avoided the Henny Penny phobia, how do you feel about entering a big building, say a theater or hotel? The fox trotters in Kansas City had no qualms. Statistically, they were better off at a tea dance than staying home. At home, a burner or a blender could radically change their schedule. Actually, it was the collapsing walkways of the Hyatt Regency which turned out to be their nemesis.

You can try to avoid an untimely demise by exacting caution or employing fancy equipment. I usually prefer the former, but have been known to flirt with junk bonds. It makes sense to be properly outfitted with reasonably good equipment for any task you undertake. However, I don't usually find the top-of-the-line stuff appealing. I am too Scotch to pay for high-priced goods and there is no guarantee that they are going to work any better. Often it is a blessing to have something wear out. Then you can switch to the latest technological breakthrough without guilt.

There was nothing fancy about the Destroyer, but it carried the "good old boy" image to an extreme. It will probably never wear out.

When it came to my bike touring, I suppose that all of my six kids thought their Dad was playing with only half a deck. Only one of them ever intimated, however, that there was some concern for my well being on a bicycle. My father, pushing eighty, took another tack. "Bob, do you think it's wise to go on these bike trips?" he would ask. "You have family responsibilities." I am sure that he had visions of a highway patrolman scraping me from the grille of a Kenworth.

"Lots of people ride bikes without trouble," I responded. "Besides, I'm a lot safer out on the highway than I am in the city or suburbs. In town, people have their mind on other things. They don't see me. They drive along, mad at the boss or worried about the fight with their girlfriend. I am a big event for a driver in the country. He says, 'Maude, look at this crazy nut out here on a bicycle.' I am very visible. Anyway, if someone should happen to do me in, the family would be well taken care of." I was insurance poor, felt I had met my obligations in that respect, and hated to be considered only as a meal ticket. It's the "he's a good provider" concept. What else does he do?

I never told Dad about the close encounters. Some were of a deliberate nature. Through the years I have had all kinds of objects hurled at me: rocks, fireworks, a whiskey bottle, beverage cans, and a folded newspaper. This happened mostly in the city. Then there was the verbal abuse, rancor and epithets from drivers who just want you off *their* road. I knew that my biggest risk was the daydreamer who never even saw me. In one brief lapse of concentration, his or mine, I could be blown away.

Arch was very outspoken about the hazards. That's his way. It kept me on guard. Thus, he did me a service. He would ask, "Where are you going on your next death ride?" I am a great worrier and I am very cautious—most of the time.

I also have faith in the Almighty. Our newly appointed minister asked me, "Do you ride alone?"

"I'm usually the only biker, but I am never alone." It can't hurt to make points with the pastor.

Actually, when as an adult my interest in bicycling was reawakened, I had little concern that there might be significant hazards. I knew that I might skin a knee. The important parts would be protected by a helmet. Adolph Weller, a valued employee and formidable bike racer, had never regained consciousness after head injuries sustained while cycling. The fact that he never wore a helmet was not lost on me. Surely, that head protection was all I really needed.

Larry McLaughlin had head protection. It was inadequate.

I have done many keen things, ostensibly for fun, which involved some risk. My own ineptitude often brought about a certain amount of frustration—and fear. I am not talking now about my professional activities, but non-work escapades to flee from ennui, and I love to work. Consider these for a study in unfulfillment:

I speared a huge grouper hiding behind some fan coral while free diving off Eleuthera. I was using a pole spear, a six-foot-long fiberglass shaft with an attached rubber tubing. I had loaned my flippers to Nancy, my daughter. My mobility in the water was not the best. The fish exploded forward after a savage penetrating thrust, ripping everything out of my hands, and darted for the open ocean. I was filled with remorse over the shark bait I had created. I never could have held the grouper. If I had, he would have dragged me to Bermuda.

Floating the Yampa and Green rivers with my brother-in-law and others in a leaking bridge pontoon, we dipped into a hole in S.O.B. Rapids. The boat flexed and catapulted our oarsman into the boiling waters. He struggled to swim to us, eyes filled with terror. We had no rope ready. He finally grabbed an extended oar. I saw a package of cigars float by and realized that my brother-in-law was overboard also. We had trouble hoisting his 230 pounds into the raft.

Stan Olson and I groped our way up the West Couloir of Longs Peak and shinnied cautiously along the northwest ridge to the summit in the blistering sun of an early June day. We were seventeen years old. We had met, en route, an experienced climber with his two young sons. He said we could tag along. We had no rope, ice ax, crampons, or knowledge of how to employ them. We had no lunch and our boots were inadequate. We were terrified. Like Burt Reynolds in "The End," we made deals with our Maker to get us off that mountain alive. We were pushing the season. Only two other climbers had recorded their names in the summit register that year, on New Year's Day. We slid down the Homestretch and Trough, braking with our elbows in the snow. We arrived at our car badly sunburned. Stan's feet were bloody.

While hunting pheasants all alone east of Otis, Colorado, I got lost in fog. I wandered in snow-filled wheat stubble, unable to sense direction in the flat light. Having been recently hospitalized, I was unsure of the limit of my strength. I cut my own tracks and stumbled around for two hours before I found a road. Then I did not know which way to go. How in hell can you get lost in the plains? I now take a compass to hunt pheasants.

Ridiculous? No. These are small incidents in a grand experience, made more memorable by the scare. I was poorly trained and poorly equipped. I suffered from a lack of physical dexterity. Perhaps I lacked wisdom. Now I had found, at last, something that *I could do*—bicycle touring. Riding a bike does not require a great degree of skill. It does take some brains, if you tour. This I had to learn the hard way. You need to plan ahead and think about water, food, shelter, repairs, roads, traffic, creatures, the elements, and injury.

I was experiencing plumbing problems, spending an inordinate amount of time in the bathroom. The problems were in me, not our house. Our family doctor told me I had an enlarged prostate gland. I asked the cause. The doctor explained that I partook of everything that was bad for my inner parts: picante Mexican dishes, Johnny Walker Red, and bicycling. (I now know the latter to have no validity.) He also added, "Oh yes, and increasing your sexual activity might help the condition." He carefully wrote out a prescription for this, in English, but it did not do any good. I'm told that a very high percentage of doctors' prescriptions remain unfilled.

I was scheduled for a T.U.R.P., which stands for trans urethral resection of the prostate. If you remember your Latin anywhere past the "All Gaul" part, "trans" means "across" or "through," and . . . Oh well, forget it. The doctors told me that there would be no open incision, but it was real surgery and as with any surgery, it involved some risks. They gave me a spinal block, which numbed my nether parts; otherwise, I was awake for the urologist's performance. Learning that he and the anesthesiologist were bikers, I rattled away about my prowess on a two wheeler. I was nervous and afraid. Later, I was embarrassed, when I found out that the urologist had ridden from Denver to Aspen, over Independence Pass, in one day.

I have a friend who went through this same operation. I learned about it after the fact, but in time to send a get-well card to the hospital. Searching for something to help him endure the indignities of the experience, I wrote this on the card, "I'm sorry that I did not know you were to have this done. I could have saved you a lot of time and money by doing the work myself in our back yard. I have all the necessary equipment. All it takes is a garden hose, Coleman lantern, binoculars, and a soldering iron."

He later confirmed my hunch that the best way to vanquish trauma when betrayed by one's body is to share the happening with humor. He said, "I passed your card around in the hospital. They all agreed you had the proper surgical instruments but were very concerned about how long you had been practicing." Picky, picky.

Other than some concern that I might bleed to death at any moment, I found the T.U.R.P. to be no big deal. They hook you up to a coat rack on wheels which supports a giant Baggie. Then you drag this assembly around the hospital corridors with pride. The real risk is to your modesty. The nurses are very up front with you.

If Anne worries about my bicycling alone, she does not show it. She tells her friends, "I can always track Bob on a trip. All I have to do is wait for the credit card statements to arrive in the mail." This would not serve me too well if I were lying in a ditch.

I had some unnerving thoughts about this possibility while biking a Colorado pass. West of Ridgway is Dallas Divide. It is not imposing as passes go, but I was there on July 20th and it was hot. I was doing my motivation thing trying to get to the only tree I could see short of the summit. I threw my bike in the borrow pit, grabbed some food and staggered up a gravel slope to seek shade. I rested under the tree, hidden from the view of drivers, and tried to recover with fruit, cheese, and water. Several cars went by and the passengers pointed to my bike. I studied its appearance. I had left things in great disarray. It looked like the scene of a serious accident. I counted thirty vehicles which passed. Not one of them stopped. I thought about that for a long, long time.

My engineering company always had an abundance of jocks as employees. They were not into team sports much, but mostly liked individual outdoor activities. We had engineers, men and women, who spent their weekends hiking, fishing, hunting, biking, and climbing mountains. We even had a sky diver. Three employees of our firm were killed in a risky enterprise. One biker and two mountain climbers died. As president of our company, it fell to me to write the parents of the most recently deceased climber. It was a difficult letter to compose. As I recall, I said something about the most rewarding experiences in life being flavored by the salt of risk. My platitude must not have helped much to assuage their grief. I never heard from them.

I know that my anxiety to get my bike on the road quickly in the mornings stems partly from fear. I just want to get at it and start cranking. In a few miles, everything is calmness. I once confessed my apprehensions to a fellow tourer. As a fireman, his knowledge of first aid and CPR would make him a valuable companion. He said, "If you were never afraid, I would not want to ride with you. Some crazy things can happen. We all do something dumb sometime. Fear could save your bacon."

Once I was in the M&M Motel in Guilderland, New York, waiting in a fit to get on the road. It was pouring outside. I wanted to skirt around Albany and Troy to enter Highway 7 toward Vermont. I had sloshed through puddles to eat breakfast in a diner across the street. Then I paced my room, alternately looking at TV and my watch. I sat down and tried to read; could not concentrate. I was forcing myself to wait until 9:00 A.M. so the traffic would subside. When the hour came I plunged into the deluge on the streets. I never should have left the motel, but I hated to waste a day sitting. In ten miles, the sky might be clear.

Trucks sprayed walls of water into me as they passed. I could barely see. When I crossed the Hudson River it was too obscure for me to admire. Dimpled sheets of water ran on the road. There was no way to identify a pothole. It was extremely dangerous, dumb, nuts. When I arrived in Bennington, my shoes and panniers were full of water. I was in the first stages of hypothermia. At maximum risk I had gained forty-six miles.

One winter I received a telephone call from an attorney unknown to me. "I have been informed that you are knowledgeable about bicycle safety and I am wondering if you would testify on behalf of a client?" the lawyer said.

"I'm not sure. Tell me the circumstances," I said.

"My client was riding his bike and he hit a hole in the paving at a bridge approach on the outskirts of Pueblo. The hole measured two and five-sixteenths inches deep by . . ." I smiled as he described the pitfall in great detail. A few hours spent delivering expert testimony had taught me that lawyers love this precise junk. It makes their argument appear to be *so* correct. "I am told that if he had crossed this groove at ninety degrees, he probably would not have fallen," he continued.

"That's true enough," I said. "How old was he?" He gave me the biker's age. The fellow was an adult. Then he launched into a description of the injuries to his client.

"I am not sure yet who is responsible, the city or the county," the lawyer said. That should not be any problem, I thought. He could name both, plus the state, plus George Bush, if necessary.

"I am sorry about your client's misfortune," I said. "But I doubt if I can be of any help to you. Any testimony from me would probably be of more advantage to the other side."

"What do you mean?"

"I feel strongly that the first rule of bicycle safety is that a biker must protect himself at all times. We would love to have perfect roads but the world isn't perfect. Everyone must accept some risks."

"I don't like your use of the word 'perfect' and the risks must be reasonable."

"Reasonable risk depends on personal bias. I would guess that your ideas on that are very far from mine."

"Would it make any difference to you if I told you how long this hole in the paving had been ignored by the highway maintenance people?"

"Not particularly. You may plead your case on that basis but the birthday of a chuckhole doesn't alter my desire to avoid it."

"I've heard enough. We *are* philosophically far apart." He thanked me and hung up. This man did not want a safety report. He really wanted a hired gun. He was determined to prove negligence on the part of somebody—anybody but his client.

About a month after that I read an article in the *Denver Post* about a different kind of accident. A twenty-year-old pedestrian on the 16th Street Mall was struck by a shuttle bus. The young man reportedly went into convulsions before being transported to a hospital, where he was listed in serious condition. A firestorm of irate opinions erupted in the press and elsewhere as the mall buses slowed to a crawl. The next day, the *Post* reported that the victim, with stitches on head and mid-section, admitted to watching a pretty girl, not the bus. "I saw this girl . . ." he recalled. "I just stopped and was looking at her. I don't think it's the bus driver's fault." A few days later the *Post* ran a letter from me on the editorial page. It said:

> Hats off to Sean Comstock for his candid explanation of an encounter with a 16th Street Mall shuttle bus. I grieve for his hurts, but it's a delight to read of someone unwilling to shift the blame.

The only problem I had with the printing of my letter was that the *Post* editors deleted my last sentence, which was, "This keen observer of the Denver scene deserves to heal quickly." Why did an editor trash my bit of encouragement? He must have considered my awkward attempt at humor to be more insulting than uplifting.

Depending on your point of view, there are risks in life which can precipitate more devastating loss than personal injury. I was in one of the riskiest businesses in the world, where an errant act could destroy reputation, finances, honor, or health. Some of my respected peers felt that these tragedies could occur to any practicing professional. Maybe so. I choose to think that such a view is tantamount to giving up. You have to work hard to stay out of trouble.

Should we take the chance at all? Let me share a writing with you. It is attributed to the Chinese moralist Confucius. He lived about two thousand years ago. Some things never change.

> *To laugh*
> *   is to risk appearing the fool.*
> *To weep*
> *   is to risk appearing sentimental.*
> *To reach out for another*
> *   is to risk involvement.*
> *To expose feelings*
> *   is to risk exposing one's true self.*
> *To place your ideas, your dreams before the crowd*
> *   is to risk loss.*
> *To love*
> *   is to risk not being loved in return.*
> *To live*
> *   is to risk dying.*
> *To hope*
> *   is to risk despair.*
> *To try at all*
> *   is to risk failure.*
> *But to risk we must.*
> *Because the greatest hazard in life*
> *   is to risk nothing.*
> *The man, the woman, who risks nothing,*
> *   does nothing, has nothing, is nothing.*

CHAPTER 6

THE PASSES

The idea had been cooking in my brain ever since the first big tour on the Destroyer. Why not bike all of the highway passes in Colorado? I studied maps. There are plenty of passes in the state, varying from paved roads to rutted old horse trails. I had driven some in a motorized vehicle, but most I had never explored. They were spread all over the western half of Colorado. This could take forever. I established some ground rules:

1) The road had to be paved.
2) The road had to cross a named pass, divide, gap, or ridge.
3) Each trip would start from Lakewood. I could cross as many passes on one trip as time would allow, but once a trip ended, I would have to start the next tour from my home.
4) If I ran out of time, it was O.K. to be rescued.

This silly little guide was only in my mind, but it deserves some explanation. My skinny-tired bike could not tolerate dirt and gravel roads. Today there are people on mountain bikes chugging all over the alpine slopes, on and off the trails. I have some reservations about the latter. We used to tear up the tundra and forest with Jeeps, testing the four-wheel-drive machines to their extremes. I was a party to this insanity for a time and I didn't have a roll bar. The new-found concern for our ecology may have saved me from myself.

I have no quarrel with mountain bikes, per se. They are beautifully designed and built. They are rugged. You could attempt Nanga Parbat with some of the twenty-one-speed bikes I have seen. They have put people back on bicycles. You can ride to work or the store through muck and slush. Improper off-road use, however, could destroy our wilderness. It is interesting to me that none of the Boulder Crazies use a mountain bike on our little tours. They aren't fast enough.

I wanted to travel roads which go somewhere. I wanted to see parts of the state which were unfamiliar to me. I also wanted to see "new" Colorado slowly, taking time to suck the beauty into my being. Someday I may ride up Mount Evans. For my envisioned goal, that dead-end ride was inappropriate.

Where does a pass start? Does it start at the road sign which states "Hoosier Pass Summit—Eight Miles"? The thought of hauling my bike in a car to that sign, or otherwise identified "bottom," did not appeal to me. Starting each trip from Lakewood seemed to be a reasonable compromise, in lieu of achieving the maximum altitude gain with a start from San Diego.

Anyone who has ridden Colorado passes on a bike knows that some of them can be a gut buster from one direction and a breeze from the opposite. If you are enchanted with the toughest direction over a pass, the data on page 45 may be of some help. Evaluation of a direction for toughness is, in some cases, very subjective. It can depend on where you start, steepness, or your tolerance for a long steady pull. Consider Rabbit Ears. I have been over it four times on a bicycle, but only once from the west, on the old orange Destroyer. I much prefer the long gentle grade north and west from Kremmling, but if you leave from Lakewood, your direction to the top doesn't matter much. The net altitude gain is the same.

When I started this crusade, time was a problem. Bicycle tours of some magnitude take enormous chunks of time. I was active in a busy profession which did not allow me to be gone on just a whim. I knew that I would encounter some severe logistic problems chaining passes together in a logical sequence. I knew that I would run out of time—and gusto. As it turned out, Anne had to rescue me twice in Durango, on the top of Douglas Pass, in Estes Park, Longmont, and Nederland. In addition to the Whitefish excursion, she has also picked me up out-of-state in Northfield, Minnesota, and Mount Pleasant, Iowa, but those are different stories. It is great to have an understanding spouse.

If you head west out of Denver for any distance, there is no way to avoid a pass. The toughest are Berthoud and Loveland, each involving an altitude gain of about six thousand feet above the Mile High City. I had already been over Berthoud, after a fashion. In 1978, I chose an easier route southwest on U.S. 285 over Kenosha Pass for a four-day tour and talked a neighbor, Ed Skinner, into making the trip with me. Kenosha's altitude is only ten thousand feet, but you go up and down plenty just to get there.

Ed and I had a fairly successful ride except we were both too inexperienced to know when we were hurting the other guy. When you ride with another person, it takes great sensitivity to avoid chafing his mind as well as his body. I was disappointed that we only got about three miles past Bailey on the first day. Ed insisted that we stop at a tourist resort for the night. We had no alternative without camping gear. I just thought we quit too early.

The next morning, we encountered a single rider who had flown his bike to Denver on an airliner from Florida. He was having tire troubles. My pump would not help; it fits Presta valves. Ed loaned him his pump which accommodates a Schrader valve, like that on an automobile tire. We left our new acquaintance behind as he fiddled with his load, but he soon passed us. Ed and I went over Kenosha with little trouble and were awed by the expanse of South Park before us. This high plain is notorious for drifting snow in the winter, but the summer wind was of no real consequence, at first. A phenomenon of biking is that the air is *always* against you to some degree, because you are creating your own breeze by your motion. Cutting a slice through the atmosphere is the worst deterrent to effective travel, not ground and machine friction. Drafting another rider reduces effort considerably.

West of Como, I could see our Florida friend ahead and I decided to push hard to catch up with him. I drew up behind him just past the base of Red Hill Pass. He did not indicate that he had seen or heard me. We both cranked slowly up the grade and then it dawned on me what he was doing. "What are you reading?" I asked.

"The *Odyssey*." I supposed it was fitting that the words of the blind bard should be assimilated by a "blind" biker.

"I would guess that highway patrolmen frown on that."

"I've never really had that problem. I read only when the country is boring or to take my mind off a big hill."

Although this act impressed me greatly at the time, I have discovered that it isn't all that hard to do. While reading, you are subconsciously aware of the white stripe below your bike. The problem is turning the pages.

Ed and I stopped to rest at the bottom of Trout Creek Pass and our companion once again left us. As we rolled toward the comforts of Buena Vista, I saw him turn in at a KOA Kampground. Ed and

I found a motel, showered, and walked to a restaurant. I was whipped and I said so. "I don't know why you are so pooped," he said. "I feel great."

"Dammit, Ed, I pulled you all the way through South Park and you wonder why I'm tired." Ed was stuck for the evening with grouchy Bob.

The next morning, it was cool and clear as we cycled south toward Salida. Deer poked their heads up from grassy meadows as we spun by. We had a great ride all the way to Canon City, where Ed talked about stopping for the night. It had been essentially a downhill day and I envisioned the possibility of our making it to Colorado Springs, which would count for a one-hundred-mile day. I conned Ed into pushing onward.

He was annoyed with me because there wasn't any place to stay in Penrose. We gulped down a beer and got back on the bikes. I mounted the crest of a long hill and saw in my mirror that Ed was fading fast. I stopped to wait.

"You had better get off that bike before you kill yourself," I said. "You're shaking like a leaf."

"What can we do?"

"Just stick out your thumb." Two cars sped by and then a pickup stopped. I propped my bike against a sign and threw Ed's in the bed of the truck.

"Aren't you coming?" Ed asked.

"No. I want to give this a shot." I talked to the driver about motels and they drove away.

When I rode past Fort Carson, I was starting to shake like a leaf. I removed my sunglasses. The light was fading. Darkness was almost upon me and I still had several miles to go. I was not well equipped for night riding, but I blundered ahead. I found Ed eating dinner in the motel restaurant. He gave me the room key and I left him to get myself together. It was all I could do to remove my clothing and stagger into the shower.

The next day we had a devil of a time trying to figure a way through the north end of Colorado Springs. Bike travel was prohibited where we wanted to go. We eventually discovered the Black Forest Road and returned to Denver via Franktown and Parker. It was a hard four-day ride which yielded only three passes, all dinky ones.

That was 1978. In 1979, I went on a tour which encompassed the toughest one-day ride I have ever made. If you head south out of

Ouray, Colorado, on a bike, you are faced with instant agony. Ouray to Durango involves three passes. The first is Red Mountain, which is an arduous 3,300 feet in elevation above Ouray. The course is at first intimidating with its abrupt incline, next claustrophobic between black rock walls, then opening to the sky on switchbacks below the summit. The road then drops down 1,690 feet through forested slopes to Silverton. Then it climbs almost as high again to Molas Divide. Another huge drop occurs before it ascends yet again to the bench of Coal Bank Pass. It's called the Million Dollar Highway. Gold ore was used for the original gravel surfacing of the road. The best views are to the east, where spectacular peaks tower above a gigantic gorge concealing the Durango and Silverton Narrow Gauge Railroad. The only reason that I could make this ride with some degree of panache was that I got in fairly decent shape riding for three days from Lakewood to Ouray. I covered the same ground which I had been over with Ed Skinner except that I kept going west from Poncha Springs over Monarch Pass (also a brute) and through Gunnison, Montrose, and Ridgway. By now I was traveling all of the time with a full complement of touring gear, including camping equipment loaded into panniers. Denver to Durango in four days on a full *or* empty bike is really trucking, no matter which route you take.

I don't ride very fast. I put in long days. I don't want anyone to think that a loaded tourer can blaze around the mountains like a rocket, just because he has a ten speed, or better. A ten speed is really an eight speed because you never put the chain in an extreme crossing pattern. It causes excessive wear and can sound like a wristwatch in a blender. At that time, I had fallen into the habit of using only six gear combinations, so you could say I actually employed only a six speed. My highest gear combination was 52/13. The low was 40/32. This is secret mystical gear head language created to impress people. It's sort of like the symbols on the back of your neighbor's BMW. What it really means is that going downhill I might travel lickety split; going uphill the seasons could change.

Any experienced cyclist will recognize that the low gear combination described above can be truly punishing, by today's standards. I now know better and have upgraded my equipment, but every ride described in this narrative was made hauling loads with no better than 40/32 on the hills. In places it was a chore.

I have burned into my memory an abundance of long sweaty climbs where I would fix on an object uproad and say to myself, "If

I can just get to that rock outcrop, then I will stop and rest," and when I reach the outcrop without a respite, then, "I survived that, let's not stop but try for the culvert ahead," and when I get to the culvert . . . Thus I talk myself to the top and don't really stop much.

I have found that the roads in Colorado are not inordinately steep. The passes may be long and high, but most of the grades are reasonable. I have no way of accurately assessing the gradient, but I would guess that few exceed seven percent. I can usually punch a big load over a long pass with two or three rest stops. I have discovered hills in Utah, California, New York, and Ohio where the grade is just ridiculous. Some I walked.

In 1980, I rode over Cameron, Muddy, and Rabbit Ears passes with the Boulder Crazies on a three-day tour and over Juniper Pass on a one-day tour, unloaded. I don't know what happened to 1981. I did not ride. Business must have been good. In 1982, I went on three long tours over twenty-one passes to clean up my commitment to Colorado. Otherwise, I might still be at this self-assigned task.

Three times I forced myself way down into southwest Colorado, once to find Gypsum Gap. It wasn't a pass at all, but west of it there is a huge hill by Slickrock. North of it is a mean grunt across the Uncompaghre Plateau which the locals call Nine Mile Hill. It was strange exciting country to me—great open vistas and the Dolores River canyons. The effort was well worth it.

My last big tour confined to Colorado was a second ride to Durango by way of a very indirect route. Our family had been invited to a wedding there and two of my kids needed to report to Fort Lewis College for the fall term. I do not recommend appearing at a wedding in cycling attire, but if Anne and Barbara and Gary could take some clothes for me along with their own, I could leave early on my bike and scratch off the remaining Colorado passes. I don't like a deadline. The word has evil connotations. If progress happens to be nil, you can end up in a struggle to make up time. This prospect gave me concern. After much soul searching and map study, I decided to allow six days for my efforts.

By the end of the fourth day, I was in Lake City, having ridden through Colorado Springs, Woodland Park, Hartsel, Poncha Springs, Saguache, and Gunnison. I had been fighting tire problems, inadvertently pinching the tubes after repair. This caused slow leaks preceding more flats. Anne and the kids were scheduled to leave Lakewood in the morning, driving the quickest route to Durango. I called her from my motel for help with supplies. She was to scurry around Lakewood and buy me new tubes and another patch kit, then search for me on the highway the next day. In retrospect, I was a big pain in the ass.

At 8:30 A.M. on August 25th, my birthday, I started up the tough incline leading to Slumgullion Pass. It was cold and cloudy, which was a blessing. The road was wet from the previous night's rain. Each time I stopped to rest I would reach down to grasp my tires, checking for satisfactory inflation. With experience, a gauge is unnecessary. It took me two hours to reach the top and the sun came out to greet my arrival. I rolled down between confining stands of timber, then through grassy meadows leading up to Spring Creek Pass. South of it, just short of the wide valley where the Rio Grande River meanders, I came to a gap in the paving and was stopped by an attractive lady flagger. Construction crews were busy. I eyed a sea of mud ahead and pondered what to do. Should I try to ride through the mess or walk? Normally I walk the bike on loose gravel. At other times, when off a hard surface, I *always* carry the bike through weedy ditches or even through grass. It prevents grief from broken glass or thorns hiding to attack my tires. It was too far to carry the loaded bike here.

"How much of this glop lies ahead?" I asked the lady.

"A mile and a half," she said.

"How would you like to have a bicycle?"

"Are you wanting to sell it?" she asked. Then she smiled. She was very pretty.

"No, I thought I might give it to you."

"That would be nice, but then how would you travel on?"

"I haven't figured that part out yet." How do I get in these predicaments?

"You can go ahead now if you like," she said gently. It was literally a down-to-earth example of having to do *something,* even though it might be wrong. I shrugged and opted to ride through the morass. That way I might at least keep my shoes clean. But I kept my toes out of the baskets, in case I started to fall. I slithered through the mud, struggling to remain upright, and never had to dirty a foot to regain my balance.

Just east of Wagon Wheel Gap, I met Anne and the kids coming toward me in our two cars, which were packed to the roofs with duds and stereos—the essentials for an education. Anne handed me the parts which I thought I desperately needed, they all wished me a "happy," turned around and bore on toward Durango. That night I stayed in South Fork at the Foothills Lodge, owned by Leo Cottrell, a biker about my age. We talked outside my room while I cleaned the mud from my machine. Later, I was feeling sorry for myself in the Fireside Inn across the road because I had been so near to my family on my birthday and now my loved ones were gone again. I talked to Chuck Wilder, the owner, and found that I was in better circumstances than he. He was suffering from a dying business. He favored me with some wine to go with my dinner. We talked jazz and listened to cool music. We both love the excitement of Woody Herman's herds and Chuck could name the Four Brothers.

Wolf Creek Pass was over before I really thought about it much. I rode on to Durango and found Anne. I had made it in six days—over eight passes. I had not used the tubes and patches she brought to me. Anne presented a memento of the passes to me as a birthday gift. It was a bracelet made from a chrome-plated bicycle chain.

At the wedding reception, I received a tribute of sorts for riding my bicycle to the ceremony. It is about 220 air miles from Lakewood to Durango. A normal driving time is about eight hours, over 370 miles of highway. The wedding guests would have questioned my sanity even more if they knew that I had ridden 550 miles for the event.

At the outset of this series of adventures, I had no precise number of trips or passes which I would attempt. When it was all over, I had completed nine trips. I counted thirty-eight hills which someone else had identified as a pass. They are listed on page 45, to which I have already referred. If you know of other passes, I don't want to hear about it. It took five years to complete this goal. I was, at the time, doing some other tours outside of Colorado. They were tough rides too, but none compare with the expeditions over Colorado passes. Nothing I have ever been compelled to do has been so rewarding. Nothing.

In the past few years, the *Denver Post* has sponsored a "Ride the Rockies" tour. The ride is a one week event which now limits the number of participants to 2,500 by means of a lottery, unlike the hilly "RAGBRAI," from which it was modeled and which accommodates many thousands of bike enthusiasts. The RAGBRAI is sponsored by a newspaper in Des Moines. The acronym stands for the *Register's* Annual Great Bicycle Ride Across Iowa. It is a week-long party in the punishing July heat and humidity. The redeeming aspect of the temperature is that it has brought the corn to a stature sufficient to hide the hoard of cyclists while they liquidate their holdings. I have participated in neither of these organized tours, but I know the territory. The Ride the Rockies tour usually includes three or four high passes, all possessing grand historic names. Conversely, the RAGBRAI tour has *hundreds* of passes, not as high but formidable, christened only by the expletives of surmounting bikers.

My rides over the Colorado passes are mapped on the following pages. The month, year, and duration of each tour is stated. All trips were made on a ten-speed touring bike. On trips A,B,F, and G, the bike was relatively empty, except for me. Not so on the other journeys. Any of the trips would make an excellent automobile sightseeing excursion, showing off the best of Colorado which is visible from a decent highway. If you *really* want to see Colorado, you must get off your butt and hike into the back country. I suppose you could ride a horse, but even it cannot take you up into the high hard stuff.

Months after Anne and I drove our cars to Lakewood from Durango, Arch and Woody and Bud, my partners in a real estate venture, secretly had a small plaque made for me. They presented it to me in a fit of jocularity at a fine dinner party, allegedly the annual meeting for our enterprise. Our wives were present. The trophy lists the number of passes I traveled for each of the five years it took. It is purportedly presented by "The National Society of Masochists." I treasure it.

"What are you going to do for an encore?" Woody asked.

"I haven't the foggiest," I said. But I knew exactly what would be next.

Colorado Passes Bicycled from Lakewood

Year	Trip	Pass	Elevation in feet	Subsequent Rides	Toughest Approach From
1977	A	1 Berthoud	11,315	1980	east
		2 Gore	9,527		east
		3 Nine Mile Gap	7,476	1978	north
		4 Rabbit Ears	9,426	1979, 1980, 1980	west
		5 Muddy	8,772	1980	east
		6 Willow Creek	9,621		south
		7 Milner (& Trail Ridge Road)	12,183	1989,1991	east
1978	B	8 Kenosha	10,001	1979, 1982	east
		9 Red Hill	9,993	1979, 1982	east
		10 Trout Creek	9,346	1979, 1982, 1987	west
1979	C	11 Loveland (and on to Montana)	11,992	1986	east
	D	12 Monarch	11,312	1991	east
		13 Red Mountain	11,008		north
		14 Molas Divide	10,910		north
		15 Coal Bank	10,600		south
1980	E	(to northwest states)			
	F	16 Cameron	10,276		east
	G	17 Juniper (Squaw adjacent)	11,140		west
1982	H	18 Cucharas	9,941	1983	south
		19 North La Veta	9,413		east
		20 La Manga	10,230	1985	north
		21 Cumbres	10,022	1985	south
	I	22 Hoosier	11,541		north
		23 Vail	10,666	1986	west
		24 Tennessee (& Battle Mountain)	10,424		north
		25 Fremont (to top and return)	11,318		north
		26 Independence	12,095		west
		27 McClure	8,755		south
		28 Dallas Divide	8,970		east
		29 Lizard Head	10,222		south
		30 Gypsum Gap	6,100		north
		31 Douglas (to top only)	8,268		south
	J	32 Ute (at Divide, there are 2)	9,165		east
		33 Wilkerson	9,507	1987	east
		34 Poncha	9,010	1991	north
		35 North ("new" Cochetopa)	10,149		east
		36 Slumgullion	11,361	1991	west
		37 Spring Creek	10,901	1991	south
		38 Wolf Creek	10,850		south

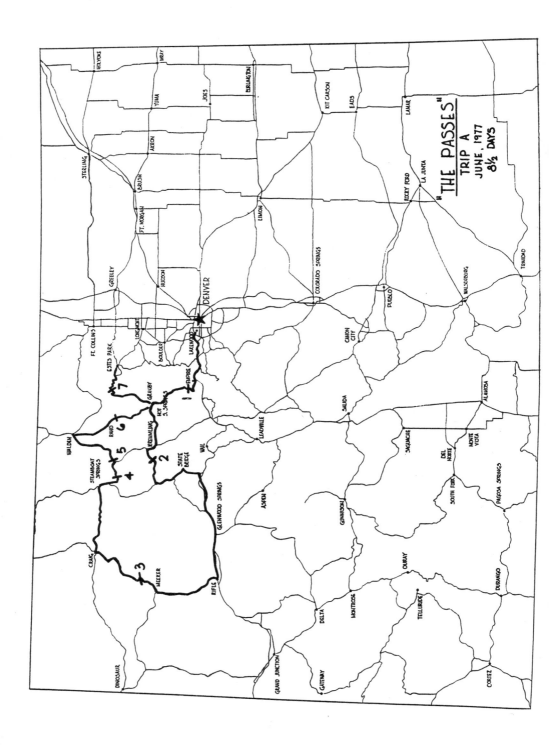

"THE PASSES"
TRIP A
JUNE, 1977
8½ DAYS

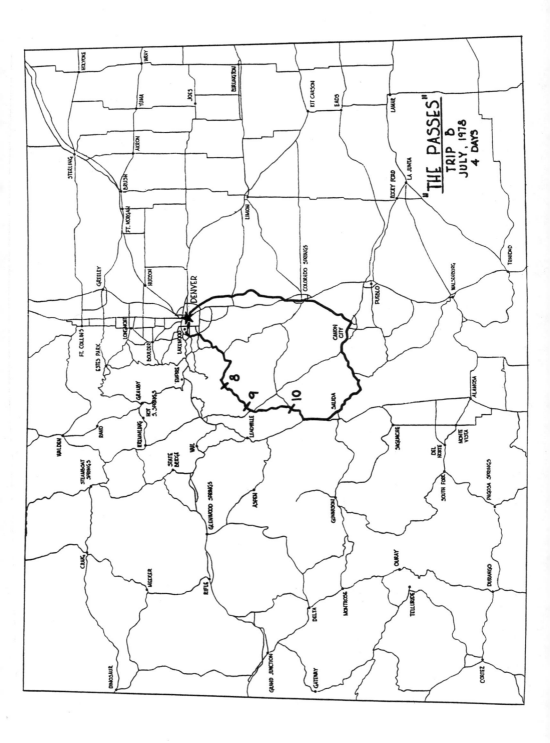

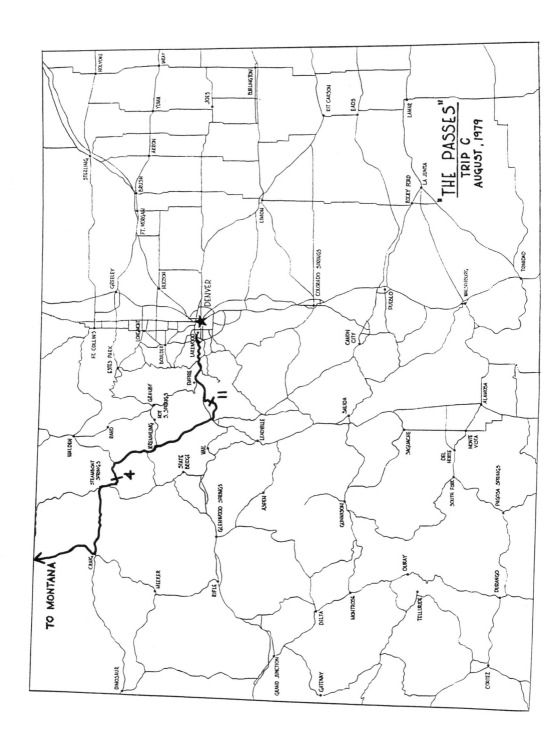

"THE PASSES"
TRIP C
AUGUST, 1979

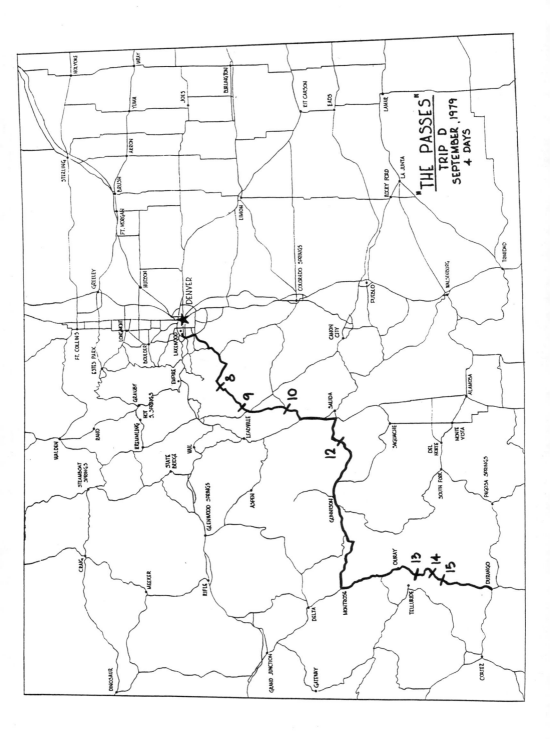

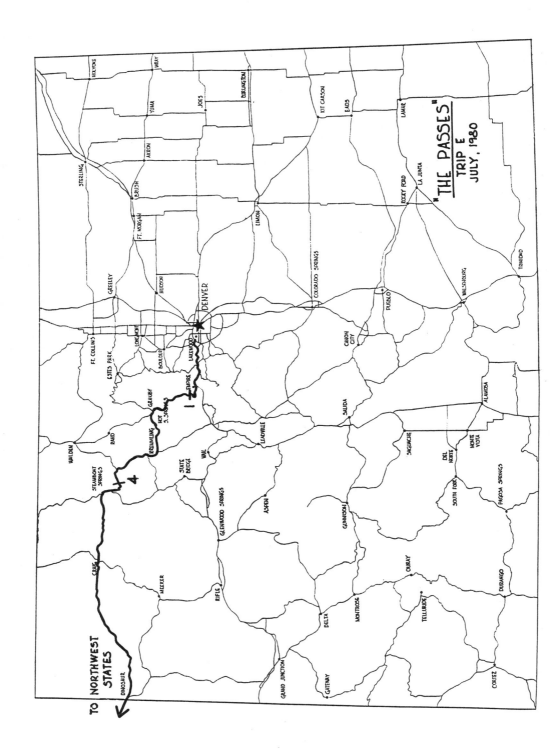

"THE PASSES"
TRIP E
JULY, 1980

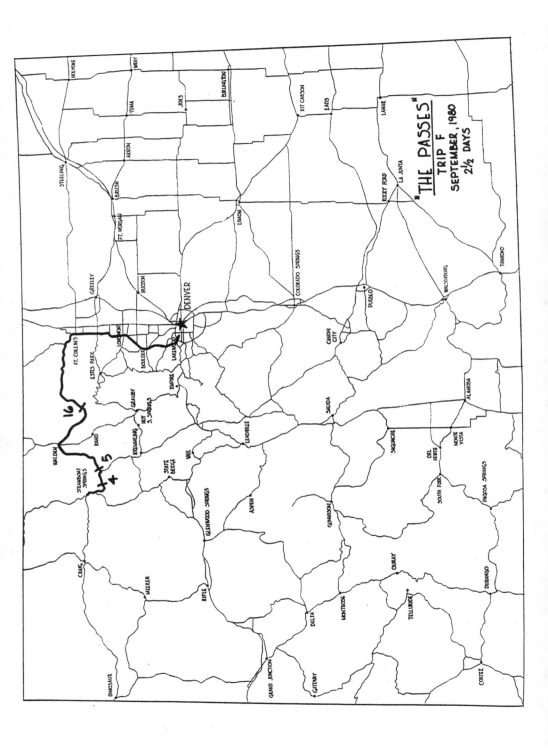

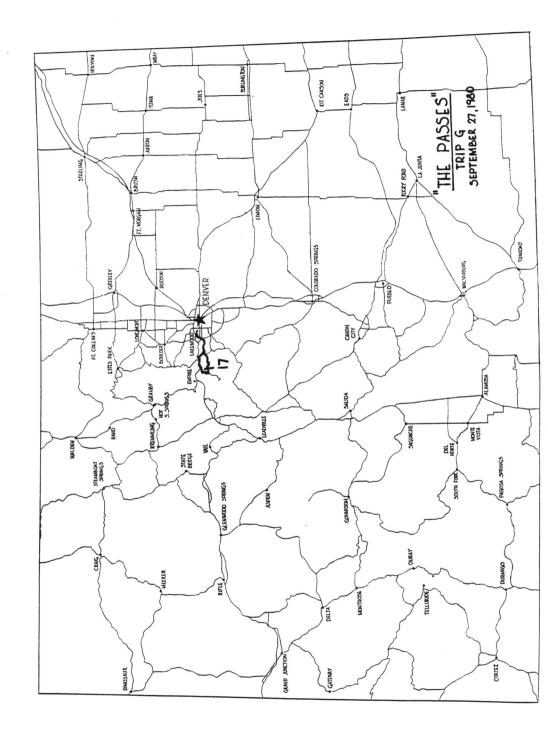

"THE PASSES"
TRIP G
SEPTEMBER 27, 1980

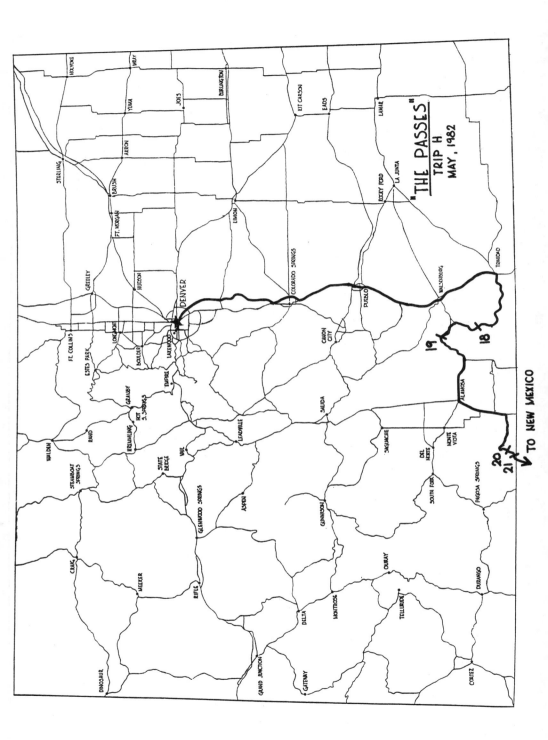

"THE PASSES"
TRIP H
MAY, 1982

TO NEW MEXICO

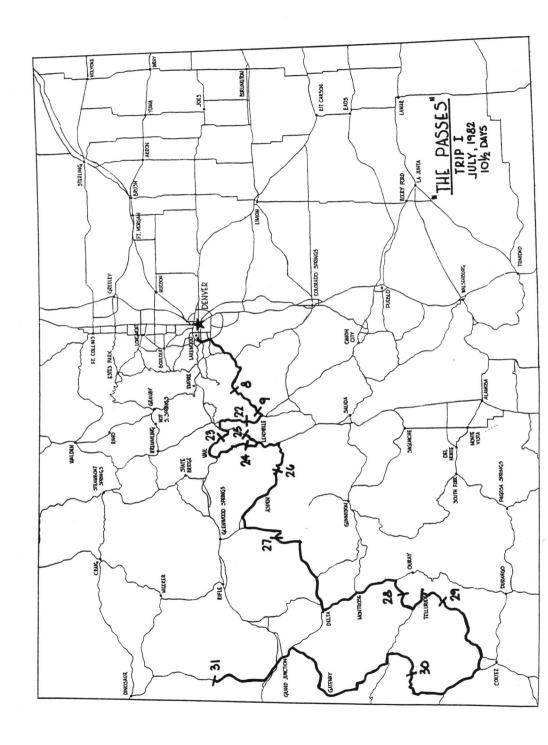

"THE PASSES"
TRIP I
JULY, 1982
10½ DAYS

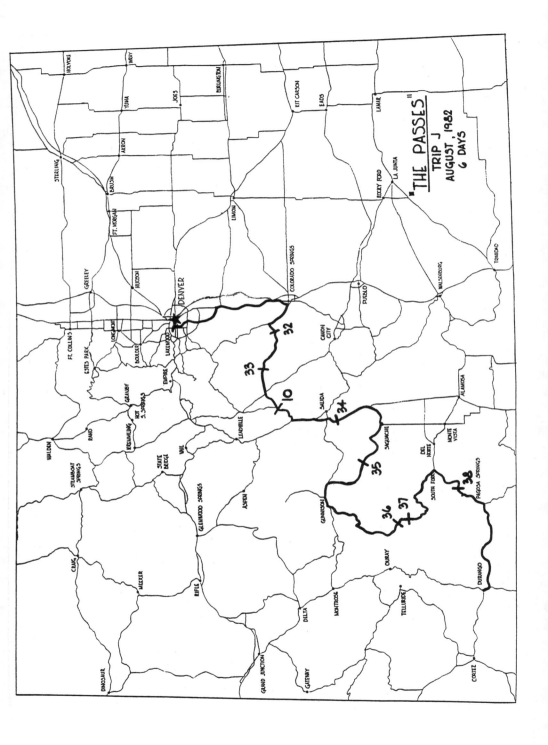

CHAPTER 7

HURT VS. PAIN

I am not into pain. It's not at all my idea of a good time. Contrary to what Arch or Woody or Bud may think, I do not have masochistic tendencies. I do not climb on that razor blade of a bicycle seat with the purpose of punishing myself. The sittable portion of a bicycle can cause great agony, but the discomfort can be dealt with. More about that later.

Hurt is something else. If you engage in any active endurance-type sport you are going to hurt. What's the difference between pain and hurt? For our purpose here, pain is something over which you have no control. Hurt you can stop instantly, and start again when and if it suits you.

My tolerance for pain is very low. When Anne digs a splinter out of my hand, the "Wow, that smarts" signals which my nerves send to my brain are at peak volume. A splinter, on my family's pain scale, is an "Owie." Any injury where blood is visible is an "Ouchie-bite." It only takes one drop to qualify. Any discomfort which might be conceivably worse is unclassified in the lexicon of misery. In my case, it is because I have never experienced such awful aches, or if I did, I either wasn't conscious long enough to endure them or inventive enough to describe them.

Based on my previous definitions, you might want to classify splinter extraction as hurt rather than pain. Anne could quit digging and the discomfort would end. Not so. Anne is a very determined surgeon. In fact, she is unstoppable.

Professional athletes play "hurt" all the time. They don't have to. They can quit the rat race and sell used cars any time it suits them. Not many do until their bodies are destroyed or the moves are gone. Pride is a great motivator. It may be that their hurt has degenerated into pain by the time a decision to retire is made. Then, as with Jim Otto of the Raiders, they struggle forever with a tortured body and there is no real rest until the final one.

My bicycling journal is a diatribe on hurt. It graphically describes sore knees, elbows, nipples, and butt. It tells about thirst, hunger, heat, cold, and exhaustion. It states when, where, and how long for just about every kind of misery you can imagine. But none of this distress was life threatening nor even very serious. Most of the time the hurt was gone in less than one day. I *could* have ended it instantly.

A big mountain pass can produce incredible, immediate hurt. But you can stop the hurt right now. You can turn around and go home. Or, you can try to ignore your burning legs and screaming lungs and git yore ass over the pass.

A thirty-mile ride can destroy a novice biker. It makes me miserable, if I have been off the bike for only a month. Everything *can* hurt, but the part of my anatomy which must be trained over and over, year after year, with thoughtful consideration and T.L.C., is my rear. If you don't go about this correctly, you can ruin a long trip. I have known two bikers who abandoned a tour because they developed saddle sores which would not heal.

True, you can search for a more comfortable saddle, padded or gel-packed, even differently shaped. This could help. But the best approach is to break in your body, not the saddle. There is no substitute for a gradual increase in the length of rides. This will also delight your other parts.

I do not wish to make this a clinical "how to" discussion for fixing all kinds of cycling hurts. The bicycle magazines do that quite well. There is, however, one other malady which plagues tourers, particularly those carrying heavy loads, which deserves comment. A lot of bikers develop knee problems pushing big loads over big mileages. It can be due to inadequate leg extension; try raising the seat a bit. A more likely cause is using gear combinations which are too high. You can get into a mind-set when shifting an unloaded bike. Certain grades require certain gear combinations. You know them. You can predict them. Added weight can trick you. You may have to adjust gearing down a little to save your body. I never saw a loaded tourer who was a classic spinner, anyway. I know that I am not.

My experiences with pain have been minimal. I never had my body slashed and seared by hot metal in a great war. I never gave birth to any of our six children and I really didn't want to. I have suffered when one of my kids did something stupid and I received a phone call from a jail or detox center. Pain doesn't have to be physical.

I tried to repair a distorted balcony rail on our house once by addressing it with a sledge hammer. I was in an awkward stance and felt a little pang after a lusty blow. The strange feeling persisted. Our family doctor at first could find no problem, but probed dutifully.

"Yeah, you're right, I can feel it now. You have a rupture."

"So what happens next?" I asked.

"You need a repair. I'll call the hospital right now. I'll send a surgeon over to look at you there. I don't do this sort of thing by myself."

The surgeon, who we'll call Doctor Dudley, went through the same drill. "No, I can't find any hernia. What did you say happened?" I encouraged him to call my doctor. He did. I was sure his second search was proving more fruitful because he had a grip on my tonsils. "Yes, there's damage. But you are too inflamed to operate on now. I'm sending you home for a week or two. In the meantime, don't lift anything over ten pounds."

"How can I go to the bathroom?" I asked. He glared at me.

I decided to bare my soul to Ed Skinner's wife, Jo, about the scheduled surgery. She was a nurse in an emergency room, saw everything gory, and knew all the doctors.

"What about Doctor Dudley?" I asked. "He seems awfully terse, no sense of humor at all."

"We call him Deadly Dudley."

"Oh, swell."

The hospital nurse prepped me and, in an effort to cheer up Doctor Dudley, I secretly taped a small piece of paper to my groin. It had a printed message, "In case of fire, lift flap." Underneath was a second message, "Not now, you crazy guy. Only in case of fire." They came to get me and wheeled me into the operating room.

When I woke up in the recovery room, there was a big bandage on me and I hurt like hell. Someone read the message on the bandage to me. It said, "The fire is out." I failed to see any humor in that at all, but was informed that the conscious operating room occupants had been in hysterics.

Jo came to the hospital that night with a friend to visit me. They had sneaked a martini in for my enjoyment. I could not even look at it.

I could hardly talk. I felt like Sonny Liston had hit me in the crotch with my own sledge hammer. I was gripping the bedrails hard, trying to hang on, and I was sweating heavily. Now, *that was pain*. Jo and her friend, sensing that my conversation lacked sparkle, left the room. I heard her say to a nurse in the corridor, "I think this man needs a hypo."

About two months later, I made a startling discovery. I had lost a jewel. It had just disappeared into the sunset. Had Doctor Dudley tied a knot in the wrong thing? I went to the family doctor and told him my concern. "That's terrible," he said. "You should go talk to Doctor Dudley about this."

I went to see Deadly Dudley. At first he was just impassive. Then he got defensive. His voice was very loud. "What are you worried about? Sex? Sex isn't in the testicles. It's in the prostate and in the head. Do you know what a eunuch is?" I allowed as how I thought I did. He yelled at me further, "Those big black dudes were castrated, man. But they weren't in the harem just to empty wastebaskets. They had plenty of *fun*! If you are so worried about losing a nad, I can put in a glass one."

So what should happen next? Should you sue the doctor for messing up your parts? Nah. How could you fault someone with such logic and sensitivity?

STRANGERS

I hadn't thought it through very carefully. If I was going to bicycle to the Olympic Peninsula to see my daughter Lisa, I should have continued on from Whitefish the previous year. Now it was 1980. I could fly to Montana and start from there, or I could start all over again from Denver. Yellowstone would be fun. A second ride down the Hoback Canyon was appealing. I had not seen a lot of Montana and could try some different roads. Let's go for it.

There was one problem. I had a sore back. It had hurt intermittently for about a month, ever since a volleyball game at Bud's house when I got hammered from behind by a teammate. Actually, we were playing jungleball, at an outdoor office party. This brand of volleyball utilizes sneaky carries, net climbing, and much gusto from beer. I went to a doctor, explained my soreness and my plans. He smiled later as he pointed to an X-ray. On my skeleton were two little knobs. "You have two broken ribs," he said. "But they are knitting nicely. Go on your ride."

Dinosaur, Colorado, was attained in three days, via Berthoud and Rabbit Ears passes. I spent nights in Hot Sulphur Springs and Craig. A tourer in Maybell was delighted with the wind. He was headed east. That worried me. It was all I could do to punch the bike to the east Dinosaur Monument station. My back was no problem, but head wind and lack of sufficient food had my body shaking. I asked a lady ranger if they had a pop machine. There was none present so I started to leave.

"Just a minute," she said, and left the counter. She returned with an ice-cold bottle of Fresca. "Be my guest." The refreshing drink pumped me up enough to ride west into town. It wasn't just the liquid. It was her attitude. She perceived my distress, responded, and it meant a lot. It happens so often, a kind word or a gentle act from a stranger. It can make your day. Now and then, you encounter hostility. Some people just don't like bikers.

In Dinosaur I met three other tourers, one from New York and two from Canada. We all gathered in a bar. The Canadians' bikes had tremendous loads. Expensive cameras with long lenses jutted from their bags. "Aren't you worried about the security of your gear?" I asked.

"We can see the cameras from here. No one will take the bikes. They couldn't lift them."

They asked me how old I was and how far I had traveled. They sensed that I was pretty wiped out even though I tried to act in control.

"You are the oldest person we have ever seen doing this," one said. "You are burning at least 7,000 calories a day with the load you carry and the miles you get. It can't be done on three regular meals. You need to eat all day long. What do you like to eat?"

"Dinty Moore stew, but it's too heavy to carry."

"Don't worry about the weight. If you like it, carry it. Try some pasta, more carbos, gorp. Suck on some fruit between meals."

I learned a great deal from these experienced bikers. They too cranked 100-mile days. They had done a couple at 170 miles, one at 200. They had mastered the energy problem but had something to learn themselves about conserving their parts. One fellow's knee was badly swollen and it hurt him a lot. They did advise me to get off the distance kick; that's not what it's all about. It would have been fun to ride with them, but they were headed south toward Rangely. They asked where I was going and I told them.

"Stock up on food in Vernal," one said. "There are no towns north and you'll have a long eight percent hill up into the Flaming Gorge."

The ride west in early morning was beautiful, with magnificent cliffs on my right. I bought groceries in Vernal and was passed by a big group of bikers heading east. Why was I always going the wrong way? The "hill" north looked awful so I stopped by a bridge to eat swiss cheese, bing cherries, and grapes. A pickup drove by and someone shouted, "You'll never make it!" I really didn't need that.

As I was resting on the long climb, a travel trailer passed and stopped. The bed of the truck pulling it was piled high with aluminum cans. A man and woman got out and started to police the area. We talked as they crushed cans and threw them into their vehicle. They were newlyweds from Oregon, just married at a Methodist church in Las Vegas. They were going to haul all of this debris home for recycling.

The world could use more people like Pete and Estelle Reed.

I spent the night camped in solitude by a gurgling little brook where I could wash and relax. I ate more swiss cheese and crackers with a cup of soup. Then I feasted on a can of Dinty Moore and some dinner rolls. My dessert was bing cherries, followed by hot tea. I wrote in my little red log book, given to me by Lisa. My notes said "camping is O.K. if on your terms and not a panic, desperate choice when totally strung out." I longed for something to read, but it did not matter. I was quickly asleep.

I had a quick breakfast of bing cherries, a can of V8, cooked rice, and a beef stick, which I pretended was bacon. On the road I passed deer and two rockchucks. Antelope were abundant, staring at the imposter. Out in the flat I saw Pete and Estelle's vehicle coming at me from a gravel side road. They waved me to a stop and gave me a package of three-minute casserole to eat later. I rode around the west side of the Gorge to Green River, Wyoming. There was no way you could get me back into Rock Springs. My impression of Green River wasn't much better. I had a verbal exchange with a motel operator which precipitated a relocation to different quarters. It cost ten extra dollars to make my point. He didn't like me or my bike very much.

Six different queries revealed nothing definitive the next morning about road 372 north to Fontenelle—paving versus gravel. I decided to chance it. The road was paved, but the asphalt had deteriorated. Broken pieces lay everywhere. There was absolutely no traffic, so I used the full road width, picking my way through the rubble. At 10 A.M. the notorious Wyoming wind commenced blowing from the west, increasing to a full blown gale as the road curved gradually to the left. Some oil tanks provided shade for lunch at the intersection with U.S. 189. It was not a great environment for a picnic. I passed the Fontenelle Reservoir and bought a root beer float in La Barge. Some sugar was needed to get me into Big Piney, my goal for the day. Now I had at least a tiny component of the wind to help me.

The Big Piney school yard looked like a good place to bed down. I saw a police car moving slowly away from me down the street. I gave chase. When I yelled the car stopped and I pulled up on the left side. I peered in at the officer and he asked, "What did I do wrong?" That made me smile.

"I was wondering if I could camp in your school yard."

"That would make some of our people tense. Better that you use the county fairground north of Marbleton." I rode on.

A car was pulling out as I approached the fairground gate.

"What do you want here?" the lady driver asked. She got out of her car.

"I'm looking for a place to camp. A police officer in Big Piney directed me here."

"You can't stay, this is private property." She glared at me and snapped a padlock on the gate.

Now I was running on nerves and anger. There were no decent sites to spend the night. It was a desert. I thought about snakes. I was very tired. A big truck passed me and I made a classic error. I neglected to look in my mirror and veered to the left. A second truck almost nailed me. "This is insane," I said. There was lifeless pasture to my right. It would have to do. The dirt was covered by cow chips which I kicked away to clear a spot for my poncho and sleeping bag. Mosquitoes attacked me. Nothing green was in sight. I could not identify anything which would serve as their breeding ground. I ate something quickly, swatting at my assailants, and crawled into the bag. I had to zip it closed over my head. I yearned for a tent through a long uncomfortable night.

The super ride down from The Rim last year had no chance of being a repeat performance. Wind was still blowing from the west. Frustrated by my slow descent, I decided to fish the Hoback. I had plenty of time to get to Jackson. Anne had given me a pistol-gripped fishing device just for bike trips. I hid my bike and set up the pseudo rod and reel, tying on a Ginger Quill. I caught two trout and quickly released each. I was kind of sneaking around because I had no license. It was too worrisome to be fun so I loaded up and rode into Jackson to look for a room. I needed a good night's rest. My body was sore from sleeping on the ground. I washed everything that night—me, my clothes, and the poncho. It was filthy.

Leaving Jackson, I spotted a foam pad lying in a ditch. I brushed it off and strapped it to my rack. It was an easy day with great views. I had breakfast at Jenny Lake and lunch at Fonda Point on the North end of Jackson Lake. When I flipped out my Golden Eagle pass at the entrance to Yellowstone, the lady ranger went berserk. She saw the pack of cigarettes in my front bag and chastised me severely, all in good humor.

The sky west of Lewis Lake Campground was ominous with shifting black clouds. Nevertheless, the fishermen were still at it. I met a red-haired fellow from California named Bob-O who was traveling with his girlfriend on a BMW motorcycle with trailer. "How much do you do in a day?" he asked. I told him. "You're going faster than we are. We're lucky to get in fifty or sixty miles. The country is so beautiful that we just have to stop and enjoy it. He's enjoying it, too." He pointed out a fisherman standing nude in the lake so he could wade out without dampening any attire.

It got cold. My camping neighbor reported snow on Craig Pass earlier that day. It started to rain. I made an envelope out of my poncho, inserting the new-found pad and my sleeping bag. The bike and panniers got some protection from a picnic table. Thunder cracked as I slid into my cocoon.

It did not rain hard. I slept soundly but was quickly chilled when I got up in the morning. I was packing fast, without any breakfast, when Bob-O walked up.

"My God, what are you doing here?" he said.

"Why? What's wrong?"

"A ranger came by last night to warn everyone about bears near the camp. A lot of people left."

"Nifty," I said.

I froze riding in dense fog to West Thumb, where I got a cup of coffee just to thaw my numb fingers. I had thought about putting socks on as mittens, but was concerned about the poor grip I would have on the handlebars. Then the great ride through Yellowstone National Park began. There were a lot of cyclists, but few loaded tourers. Old Faithful spouted dutifully five minutes after I rode up. I did not stop to see the myriad of bubbling places, only to look at animals. We did not converse much because other people were around.

I had a flat tire, the first of many to come, north of Hebgen Lake. After a quick change to a new tube, I pushed on to the Quake Lake visitor center, where I encountered several bikers from Australia. I inadvertently insulted one young lady because I did not properly identify the flag on her packs. I thought she was from England. It's too bad that I didn't listen to her speak first. She told me that there were many more in her party, struggling east toward us through severe wind. Wind from the east? I thought it best not to tell her how delighted I was.

When I entered a great valley, I saw the rest of the Aussies. They were strung out for miles, fighting their way up a slight grade. I streaked past them. The wind was actually more from the southeast, right at my back. I hardly had to crank. Ahead, though, loomed dark clouds in the Madison and Gravelly ranges on the east and west sides of the valley.

I stopped for a beer in a tiny wayside emporium. The lone bartender, a huge muscular type, addressed me. "Which way are you headed?"

"North."

"The Aussies are going the right direction. You're going to get wet."

"That could be true, but I have a tail wind." He shook his head. You could tell that he thought bicyclists were nuts.

It was getting dark and I could not make it to Cameron. I prepared my bedroll about one hundred yards east of the highway on a soft grassy field. The wind had abated. I admired fantastic sunset colors on rain sheets to the east. Dark clouds enveloped the mountains to the west. I settled in to wait for the rain. It never came. It was like Moses had parted the waters for me to ride down this superb valley.

The next day, I really got discouraged. It seemed like I was spending all my time changing and repairing tubes. Early on I discovered that it was really a tire problem. They were about shot. As always, the back tire was the worst. Bare fabric showed between patches of smooth rubber. I considered going toward Bozeman to find a bike shop, but I didn't think I could get there before stores closed. It was also Saturday. Nothing would be open the next day. My plan of going to Helena had to be abandoned. I pushed for Whitehall in a fit of depression, fixing flats all the way.

That night, from Whitehall, I called a bike shop in Butte to see if I could get tires and tubes on Sunday. The proprietor said, "You have a pass to go over. When you get in town, give me a call and I'll come down to the shop." He gave me his home phone number. The next day, Roger Baker opened Fritz's Bike Shop to sell me tires and tubes. His gracious act saved me a whole day. I decided not to change tires until I had to, with my next flat. I rolled the new tires in a figure eight, popped them into a circle, and attached them to my load with bungie cords. As luck would have it, my old tires then decided to stay inflated for many more miles.

After a fast morning on Interstate 90, I turned east on U.S. 12 to enjoy the great scenery along the Little Blackfoot River. I camped at the Nevada Creek reservoir, north of Avon, by a lone little pine tree near the dam spillway. I threw down my bed and just crapped out for a while. My leg muscles hurt good. It felt great to go hard. I admired the beautiful green valley and river and sunset to the west. Montana was terrific.

Highway 83 was a *terrible* bike road. The south half was old, with broken paving and no shoulder. Semi's were running both ways and

I had my first experience with logging trucks. They really test you, allowing very little room when they pass. North of Golden, Colorado, there is a road which can be a biker's nemesis. It is better now, but we used to say, "Pray for me. I ride 93." In Montana you just substitute 83 for 93. I also had my first taste of Mount St. Helens. I mean that literally. Ash from the eruption was drifting down out of the sky and I could not avoid sucking it in.

My back tire, running on the cords, finally gave out at about four o'clock in the afternoon. I had a moderately greaseless tire change in the forest, glancing around occasionally for bears. I called Audrey and Dean Dahlgren, who live in Bigfork, from Swan Lake, where I intended to camp. She told me to ride on in. I passed an oil slick in the lake where a tanker had plunged, but learned later that the driver had survived. I arrived in Bigfork, soaked with sweat. Audrey fed and watered me after I went for a dip in Flathead Lake. I slept soundly on the cushions of their boat as it rocked in the water. The mileage for the day was about 130.

It's only a short jaunt to Whitefish from Bigfork, but I was forced to leave the road three times to avoid logging trucks. I stayed with my son Bruce for four days. I cleaned my bike and mounted the other tire. That took the better part of a day. In Whitefish, I bought a hooded sweatshirt and a small tent. Then, eager to get going, I studied maps. If I could make it to the Olympic Peninsula in eight days, log trucks could be avoided on two weekends. The primary road I selected was Highway 20 through Washington, which I learned later was the North Cascades Route.

The first day, I journeyed north to Eureka, which is nine miles from Canada, then west and south along Lake Koocanusa to Libby. The lake must be one hundred miles long; I rode along it for about fifty. I could feel the effect of the four day layoff and the added weight of the tent and full load of water I was lugging. It was a good thing that I carried the water, because the superb paving of Highway 37 was far from the lake and there was no civilization.

At Libby I entered U.S. 2 which goes through Bonners Ferry, Sandpoint, and Priest River, Idaho. Once in Washington, I rode Highway 20. This is a windy and windey way to get to the West Coast. There are a number of passes and very punishing long hills. Heat in the valleys can destroy you. North of Cusick, ash was dumping out of the trees so badly that it made my teeth grit. I could not cut the scum with water. A can of Fresca helped.

In the empty "Scenic View" campground on top of Sherman Pass I was stumbling around afoot trying to recover from the climb. On the ground was a leather billfold. I picked it up. Inside was about forty dollars, credit cards, and a driver's license. I stuffed it in one of my bags. Eating a roast beef sandwich and bowl of soup in Republic, I pondered over the wallet. What if I crashed and someone misidentified me because of it? What if someone thought I stole it? Should I carry it all the way? Should I try to call the owner or just mail it?

The hill out of Republic took my mind off the lost billfold. I was not mentally prepared for two passes in one day. My eight-day schedule looked to be in jeopardy. I finally topped out on a lonely high grassy valley and saw a tiny post office in the town of Wauconda. I parked the bike and entered. Inside was a busy lady who asked if she could help. Her name was Elva Helm. I asked her if she could assist me in mailing the wallet to its owner. She rummaged around, searching for wrapping paper and string.

"Do you think it would be proper if I used his money to pay for the postage?" I asked.

"I would certainly think so," she replied. She wrapped and I recorded names. When I thanked her and started for the door, she said, "You made my day." When I got back to Colorado, there was a grateful letter from the wallet owner waiting for me with a reward check for ten dollars. This didn't seem quite right, somehow. I wrote a check for five dollars and mailed it to Elva.

Coming out of the Okanogan Valley, I sweat buckets. Loup Loup Pass was a mean mother. I had ridden thirty miles before breakfast with terrible hurt in my right knee. After I ate, my knee was fine. Strange. This had happened several times. Stop to rest and the hurt goes away or something pops into place. I wanted to get up the east side of Washington Pass a goodly distance before I quit for the day, so I pushed hard to Lone Fir Campground, which had huge rocky crags above. There I had a sponge bath with water heated on my stove and cooled two cans of beer in the nearby stream. I met a biker from Denver, John Price. I also met a lady named Gail and her playful German Shepherd, Mary, who came over to introduce themselves. Gail asked if I was married. Mary just looked at me. I said yes.

I cooked dinner and turned in. That night I woke up, gazed at the stars and smoked a cigarette.

I started at 6:15 and was on top by 7:30 A.M. It was a good hard crank. Rugged snowy peaks were around me. There was a mammoth monolith of rock just south of the pass. It was cold. I put on my new sweatshirt, long pants, and a jacket, then rode into the trough leading to Rainy Pass. Soon I was in *huge* trouble. I started to shiver. The wind chill going downhill was freezing me. I could not control the bike. Spasms shook my arms. I stopped but it was cloudy, so I stood there and shivered. I got back on the bike and tried to crank in reverse, to build up body heat. I just could not think and I had to get *down*.

The trouble with hypothermia is that your mind goes. I had everything I needed: tea, soup, stove, sleeping bag, tent. I just could not comprehend what was happening and I wanted desperately to be off that mountain. I had burned every calorie in my body. It's lucky there was no traffic. I was all over the road before a patch of sunlight saved me. I stopped to soak in the warmth, then rode slowly down to Ross Lake.

I called Jan and Bill Clevenger from Burlington to see if I could crash at their house near Sequim. The ride down Whidby Island was a lot like England would be, I thought. Maybe it was the weather. It rained all day. I tried riding in my poncho, but it did not breath so I was quickly soaked with sweat. I was also concerned that the whipping fabric would blow into the spokes. I decided it was better to get wet from the rain and took the poncho off. At Deception Pass, the cross wind was so severe that I could not chance a good look, and it was raining hard. This pass is a tidal current, not a high road. It looks like rapids in a powerful river. I took a ferry to Port Townsend and was soon in the Banana Belt. At Clevengers', I embarrassed myself before them and their other guests, stowing away delicious salmon and other good food like it was my last meal.

Before anyone else was up, I sneaked out. This will be a long day, I reasoned. U.S. 101 is generally a good road, but at Crescent Lake there was a problem. A big sign warned bikers about the log trucks and recreation vehicles. I had made my eight-day goal, it was Sunday and I didn't need to worry about the former. However, I was about to encounter a new hazard. What the sign should have said is:

> There is absolutely no shoulder on this road. We have placed raised reflectors to mark the edge. Inside the reflectors are motorized vehicles. Outside the reflectors are fish. You are about to die!

About three miles around the lake, the shift cable to my rear derailleur broke. I had to make a run for it in high gear. It was a frenzied sprint for about seven more miles. I was hemmed in by the dumb reflectors and had to be very wary of vehicles.

In 1988, I drove this route in a car just to see how bad it was. It's all changed. The road has been widened and repaved. It's no big deal for a biker because they now have a nice lane to the right of the reflectors. The signs, which I think are the same, really say:

BICYCLISTS READ NOTICE

Please use caution while traveling the next ten miles. The road is very winding with no shoulders. Many trucks and recreation vehicles use this section of road. Please pull off the roadway and allow traffic to pass whenever possible. Remember: sight distance is limited because of the curvature of the road and the speed difference between vehicles and bicycles may cause vehicles to come upon bicycles without warning.

Under this message someone had scrawled:

You're second class in this state.

Under this was:

BUT ALIVE!!

At Fairholm I spent two hours trying to devise a cable clamp. A nice gent there, seeing my distress, brought me a bucket of nuts, bolts, and junk which are like solid gold to any would-be mechanic. I got the gearing cinched in to my second smallest sprocket, mounted the bike, and stood up to crank the hill to the west. I could not make it, had to get off and walk. I could manage fairly well on the flat and over gentle grades, but the chain popped onto the smallest sprocket when I crossed a bridge expansion joint. In Forks, I found two other tourers at a hamburger stand, one of whom sold me a spare cable for a dollar.

I stayed four days with Lisa and her husband Gene in Clearwater, Washington. Gene was a logger. He made a living salvaging cedar from stumps of trees which had already been cut. Cedar was so scarce that they re-entered clear cut areas to saw "bolts" which were bundled and carried to trucks by helicopter. The bolts were later split into shakes for roofing. Gene told me that about two hundred log trucks came through Clearwater in one day, and it was not on the primary coast highway, which has even more trucks. The log truck drivers called bicyclists suicide bunnies.

It took two and a half days for me to ride to Portland. By then I was very spooked by the trucks. A lot of the trip was through fog. My glasses would mist over so that I could not see. When I removed the glasses I lost the advantage of the attached mirror and the passing trucks terrorized me. Some of them were tandems, which are called "mule trains." The first section would go by and I would think, "I cheated death one more time." Then the second section would blast past, a total surprise.

I found where my son Danny lived in southeast Portland. He stayed with an elderly gentleman in a ramshackle house where they both barely survived. I knocked on the door and stared at the untrimmed shrubbery and trees. Dogs barked inside. Danny answered my knock but he did not invite me in. The old man would not let him, he said. I looked at Dan, who was barefoot, unkempt, and filthy. He had cuts and sores on his arms and legs. His condition was very depressing. I invited him to lunch and we walked to a restaurant. I could not tolerate being with Dan long, it pained me so to see his dire circumstances and dirty, damaged body.

I called an airline from a pay phone for a reservation to Denver. Then, feeling very blue, I decided to ride to the airport and take pot luck. When I got there, I found that a plane was leaving in one hour. The ticket agents insisted that I box the bike for shipment. They furnished the cardboard and tape, but I had no wrench properly sized to remove the pedals. I loosened the handlebars, turned them parallel with the front wheel and just crammed the thing into the box as best as I could. It looked strange, with bulging sides, but they accepted it. After washing quickly in the men's room and changing to long trousers and a fresh T-shirt, I checked my panniers and other bags through the baggage counter and ran for the gate to my plane.

I sat next to a well-dressed attractive young woman. I had the window seat. Flecks of sunburned skin dusted off my arms onto my dark blue jogging pants. I was sweaty from the ride and the run and the exertion of packing in a hurry. I felt that my appearance deserved an explanation but decided to say nothing. Why should she listen to a tramp? Just after we took off, a voice came over the loudspeaker, "Good afternoon, ladies and gentlemen. This is your captain speaking. Our flight time to Denver will be one hour and fifty-four minutes." My eyes welled up with tears. I looked out the window, then down at my soiled trousers and sunburned hands.

"Is something wrong?" the lady beside me asked.

"No. Nothing, thanks." It had taken me twenty-three days to ride 2,247 miles. I would make the return trip home in two hours. I could not even attempt to explain my feelings to her.

It had been a grim day.

THE SALUTE

Compared to the three-fingered Boy Scout salute and the two-fingered Cub Scout salute, the biker's salute is more efficient. It delivers a succinct message with minimal dexterity and muscular exertion. It should not be delivered capriciously, but retained in order to produce the maximum effect for those most deserving. If you are a novice biker, you may need some help in identifying the other kinds of travelers who merit an explicit salutation. There are three distinct types.

The first is a young lass driving her boyfriend's pickup. She has an identity problem. She suffers from a hormone imbalance which is corrected by the roar of the vehicle. It will have no muffler. It will also have dual rear wheels, oversized, and mirror brackets extending thirty inches from each side of the cab. She has no idea where these portions of the truck are and is trying to make that determination by passing you as closely as possible. Upon completing the pass, she will look in her mirror for you. If you are no longer visible, then she knows that she has established boundaries. Obviously, it will be difficult for you to extend a salute if this is the case. Otherwise, give her a nice signal to award a superior effort.

One word of caution. Always look carefully at the gun rack in the rear window of the truck. If it contains an Uzi, don't bother with the salute.

The second type is not a driver, but the passenger to his right who screams an unintelligible epithet at you at the precise moment their vehicle is adjacent. He will have a can of beer in his hand, unless he has chosen to forfeit the recycling benefits, and lofts it in your direction. If you can recover your composure, give this fellow a nice salute. He will invariably grin at you in return. Don't bother to gesture to the driver, because he will not see you. He will be busy pulling on a bottle of Jim Beam.

Type three consists of two senior citizens out for a Sunday drive in their Essex. They are extremely courteous and would not dream of passing you. They have been right on your tail for eight miles. They have read in the papers about bicycle safety and they don't want to impale you on the hood ornament of their freshly polished car. That might distress you and them. They are intelligent people who understand the principles of physics. They are thoughtfully waiting for you to fall down so that they can run over you with all four wheels, equally distributing the weight of their vehicle to all parts of your body through the soft fat tires. Help make their day.

The "inverted salute" is handy for people whom you ascertain have a brain deficiency which causes them to read upside down. I have had great success with this when mooned by high school kids from the back of a school bus.

There is a rather exotic gesture, different from the conventional salute, which I reserve for logging truck drivers, particularly those who are pulling tandems. They seem to have an educational disadvantage because they either can't count the number of trailers in their rig or can't remember whether they attached both at the last stop for pie and coffee. Lacking the benefit of this knowledge, they will invariably cut you short as they pass. Drivers with this handicap deserve our compassionate recognition and understanding. Bless them, but only if you have considerable bicycling experience and can ride without touching the handlebars. The gesture requires two free arms.

Practice the salute and gesture at home before a mirror so that you can learn the nuances and deliver a superior performance. Other cyclists will love you for it. If this habit can grow, bikers everywhere will have multiple opportunities to signal happy highway greetings.

Next Chapter: "How to Remove Broken Teeth from that Funny Little Thing Hanging Down in Your Throat"

I had just returned from a bicycle trip of over three thousand miles to the East Coast. There had been plenty of opportunities to hail fellow travelers with the salute. Not so with the gesture. It is more appropriate in Montana, Idaho, Washington, and Oregon.

A quick fishing break was in order. I knew where fish were positively attainable, although it involved a twenty-mile drive to the top of

Trail Ridge from our cabin and a steep hike down to the headwaters of the Poudre River. I was on the river by 11:00 A.M., flexing my rod toward sparkling riffles at the head of shadowy pools. It was a lovely day, but very windy, which affected my casting accuracy which isn't all that great in calmness. Twice I reached over the bank to retrieve a fly caught in the willows.

By noon I had five nice brook trout, "good eatin' size," which means they were pretty dinky but I never learned to fish with bait. I could see a trout run for cover every so often, spooked by my flailing. I sat down on a gravelly bar to eat my lunch and give the fish a break. I downed a sandwich, nectarine, and cookie. Then, still seated, I cast upstream once and downstream once into a quiet pool. These moves produced two more keepers. I stood, pulled my straw hat down tightly to deal with the wind, and sneaked upstream attempting to cast.

There was a good tug. It was the biggest thing I had on the line all day so I set the hook neatly. What I caught was me. The fly was buried in my right hand. I sat down to survey the situation, pulling my Swiss Army knife from my pocket. The barb was invisible. I probed and tried to cut flesh with a blade and then the scissors, but that was an "owie" and my hands started to shake. The thought of severely stabbing myself and bleeding profusely was a strong deterrent to outdoor surgery. It was going to be a long climb out of the valley.

I cut the leader, attached a new fly, and fished until I caught one more trout. It started to rain, but I took time to clean the fish at streamside. The hike out was no problem, except for a twinge now and then when my hand brushed some pine needles. I got in the car, drank a warm beer, and headed home.

Anne looked up when I entered the cabin. "How did you do?" she asked.

"Fine. I got my limit. I think I need to find a doctor." I smiled and held up my right hand in a friendly salute. She looked at the Rio Grande King stuck in the tip of my middle finger.

"It's poetic justice," she said.

CHAPTER 10

MOTIVATION

I laugh when I consider some of the events which shaped important decisions in my life: education, marriage, career, location. I suppose it's the same for everyone. Does mere chance control our destiny? It's possible. I would like to think, however, that my own ambitions were somewhat responsible for any successes achieved. We may have inner drives, but friends and relatives can cajole us onto another path if they choose. In my case, these people would not have to be particularly tricky. They would just have to know what turns me on and, now that I am older, that I am often cross-motivated. When I was younger, a mentor would not have to be smooth at all.

As a youngster, I was a studious, skinny, frightened kid. If someone asked my opinion about professional athletics, I would expound on the terrible waste of a person's life. Secretly, I longed to be a jock, for which I was ill-equipped. It was not that I had made the profound discovery that all of life is a big game. I just suffered the ignominy of never owning a letter sweater.

I wasn't totally spastic. I could swim fairly well. One summer I worked as a lifeguard. I played what was called sandlot football but I confess to never seeing a lot of sand. I ran up and down court in church league basketball games. In my town this simple endeavor required supreme bravery because the YMCA basketball floor contained a building column within the boundary lines. But I was not a varsity athlete. I was considered a "brain." Little did they know.

I was raised in Sioux City, Iowa. Sioux City hasn't grown a lick in fifty years, but I think it was a good place for me to grow up. My father and grandfather were portrait photographers and they were very good at it. They worked long debilitating hours and I never saw my father except when he took mom and me to the weekly movie on Friday night and church on Sunday. He quickly fell asleep in both because he was so exhausted.

For two brief stints we moved to California for my mother's health. During one trip west my Dad took us over to see Boulder Dam. I showed some interest. When my father later discovered a stunning aerial photo of the structure taken by one of his coworkers, he had it framed and brought it home to me. It was nice, so I hung it in my room, but I never dreamed that the photo of a concrete monolith holding back the sparkling waters of Lake Mead would dictate the course of my life. My Dad would introduce me to his friends, "This is the heir to the Voiland millions. He has a head on his shoulders and is going to be an engineer, not a pigeon-toed picture taker." I would cringe and try to smile. I became an engineer all right, but I never designed a damn dam. When I get discouraged about my own kids' seeming lack of direction, I reflect that my enrollment at Iowa State to study Civil Engineering came about largely because I could not think of anything better to do. I knew one thing for sure. I didn't want to be a photographer.

Upon graduation from college, I came to Denver to work for Milo S. Ketchum, a consulting structural engineer. It was the worst paying job of the four offers I had, but I didn't know diddley so I got way more than I was worth. My Dad was distressed that I hadn't gone to work for someone he had heard of, a big corporation like American Bridge or Swift & Company. I assured him that I could learn more with Milo and he seemed to accept that. Actually, my primary reasons for coming to Denver were to use the cabin in the mountains and to chase my wife-to-be's sister, Else.

It didn't take long to find out that I had more in common with Anne than Else. Their mother loved to tell me that she was so happy I had brains enough to go for the cake rather than the frosting. Their father was a Danish mechanical engineer, in the true sense. By that I mean that he designed tools, not air conditioning and plumbing. He was the second genius I was to run across. The first was Milo. There haven't been any others.

I had a fun, rewarding career designing structures for buildings. At twenty-five years the ardor started to fade. At thirty-five years, motivation was almost nonexistent. I won't discuss the reasons here. I got on the Destroyer to escape, and one trip led to another. I did not have to learn to ride a bike at age fifty. I learned when I was a kid and, like they say, you never forget. Then, a bicycle was just a means of getting from one escapade to another. It wasn't the main event. The Destroyer taught me that I would have to learn to *really* ride a bike.

There aren't many things which I do in moderation. I know this can be my undoing, any one of several ways. The family doctor has warned me about these excesses, but initially I think he was only aware of and concerned about my biking. He once asked me if I was on an ego trip. The question at first angered me, but I guess he was on track. If setting goals, meeting them, and having a great deal of satisfaction in the conquest is an ego trip, then I qualify.

The neat thing about a big bike trip is that the goals are so achievable. All you have to do is keep plugging away, and you get there, sooner or later. I would prefer it to be sooner. If you want to get home to watch the Super Bowl, you better reel in more than fifty miles a day. It ought to be twice that. It's all up to you, baby. No one can change the rules on you.

The *ride* on the bike is what it's all about. Sure, the scenery can be awesome. You feel good all over with the exercise. You may like camping. To me, it's the means to an end. There could be some adventure, but I believe a paved road is reasonable evidence that the area has been explored. The people along the way are usually wonderful, but you don't meet a lot of folks. It's not that you don't want to. It takes a lot of time to be an ambassador and it is unlikely that a crowd will be gathered along the roadway just dying to shake your hand. Now and then your mettle will be tested by adversity. A little bit of that will go a long way. These are all great motivators, but to me they are secondary. Primarily, you are out there to crank a lot of miles.

The farther away from home you tour on a bicycle, the better you feel. It's not that you are attempting to leave an undesirable place. Home is a good place. The idea is to ride your *bike* away, not a motorized vehicle. In addition to the toning of your body from exercise, your mind is being stretched. An aura sets in. Mundane matters dissolve and there is a renewed acquaintance with important truths forgotten. Giant strides are taken beyond old familiar horizons into the vastness of God's handiwork.

Friends ask me why I don't like to throw my bike on a car or plane for transport to some unknown state or country and *then* cycle around. I tell them, "That's cheating," and they look at me as if I were deranged. To follow their suggestion means to forego the mystique when you say to yourself, "Wow, this is really something. Look at this *new* stuff. I'm out here six hundred miles and all it took to get here was a few repetitive motions with my scrawny little legs."

My road bike will fit inside our Saab, without removal of a wheel, but I detest driving my auto fifty miles in order to bicycle thirty. I will do so only to enjoy the company of friends. The true utilization of a mountain bike, more properly described as an all-terrain bike, usually requires that city folk haul the thing on or in their car. That's O.K., but mountain bikes are really not my bag. More about that later.

Is this the last hurrah for an old fart? Maybe so.

My father and I had similar military experiences. We both enlisted to become pilots and we both missed a terrible war, World Wars I and II. Along with several other kids from the Midwest, I was directed to merge with a Navy V-5 unit of easterners at Swarthmore College in Pennsylvania. We were allegedly the "cream of America's youth" and we all had this burning passion to fly off of carriers. At least for a while. My closest pals were from Colorado. I envied their proximity to the mountains which I suspected would some day be my domain. I spent a lot of time with Jim Richards from Rocky Ford, Floyd Wesley Wilcox from Canon City, Gene Meakins from Fort Collins, and Walt Smith from Denver, who played great piano even then. None of them, to my knowledge, were motivated to stay in the service. I know for a fact that one of our prospective "zoomies" did have a career as a naval pilot and officer. He was a quiet young man from Greeley whom I knew as "Cal" Swanson.

Following Swarthmore, I was sent to Memphis to fly and solo a Stearman biplane, the *Yellow Peril*. An instructor gave me "poor" and "average" grades on every maneuver but one—spins. Those I executed with some trepidation, but he delivered a mark of "good." I don't know why. I would get locked in fascination with the whirling earth below and had to be startled into action by a scream through our one-way communication tube, "Rudder, dive and pull, Buster! That ground is hard!" I always had a little problem with depth perception, but this was ridiculous.

The pilot instruction in Memphis was called Selective Flight Training. The Navy had discovered that they were spending barrels of money on young men to send them to college and Preflight School only to find out during Primary Training that many of the youngsters had no aptitude for flying. They would "wash out" and all of the dollars were wasted. In their belated wisdom (it took all of World War II to figure this out), the Navy put cadets through Selective Flight Training before Preflight to save the expense of the latter experience for some. I wondered why they did not check out our potential flying skills before sending us to college. They might have saved even more money.

We received ten hours of dual instruction in the Stearman and then we were supposed to solo. We swam some and worked at chores on the tarmac some but mostly we sat around in the ready room playing "Hearts" for a penny a point, waiting for conditions to be right for us to strap on a parachute and go fly.

I was a jewel on the tarmac. An F4U landed and I was to direct it to a parking spot because a pilot cannot see very well around the cowling while taxiing. I pointed at the wheel to brake and motioned him forward with my other hand. Before I could stop him with both hands upraised and a slash across my throat directing him to cut the engine he rolled forward right up over the wheel chocks and lurched to an ignominious halt. The pilot climbed out of the cockpit and glared at me as he walked away.

I was fueling a *Peril* astride the top wing when I did something goofy with the hose nozzle. Gasoline poured into the cockpit below and I was disgraced.

The day I was to solo I did everything wrong. I was very nervous and it seemed that I was either hesitant or overcontrolling each maneuver. I was afraid to let the machine just do its own thing and direct itself. The check pilot talked to me a lot, trying to calm me down. Finally he wiggled the stick and said, "I've got it," and he landed the plane on one of the tiny outlying practice airfields which always seemed to have a menacing grove of trees at the ends of the runways. I figured he was going to read me out, but good. He got out, climbed up by me and yelled in my ear, "I probably shouldn't do this, but I'm going to give you a crack at it. If something looks wrong to you, take a waveoff and go around again. If you splatter this airplane I will never forgive you. Good luck and for God's sake, be careful." With that bit of encouragement he stepped down.

I taxied down to get in line and took off with no problem. It was very scary thinking about landing but comforting not to have someone shouting at me. There would be no one except myself to guide the aircraft between the trees if I overshot an approach, which I was prone to do. I noticed that other planes were now landing from a different direction, which puzzled me. Then it dawned on me that the wind had changed direction. I stayed in the pattern and guided the Stearman down without incident.

I taxied toward my check pilot when this routine was complete. He was all smiles as he climbed up into his cockpit. Then he asked, "Are you fastened in really tight?" I nodded in the affirmative. He took off with full power and immediately executed a snap roll. He was probably surprised that I did not fall out. At two hundred feet my parachute would have been a late bloomer. Then he dove the plane at two instructors waiting on the ground for their students. I looked at my mentor and he was laughing at them as they scrambled. He was just tickled that I had not ruined his career by killing myself. A third of my class did not make the grade. They washed out.

I was sent on almost a month's leave to wait for Preflight School to commence. I drove out to Estes Park from Iowa and hiked the trails in Rocky Mountain National Park. I also bushwhacked around from peak to peak enjoying the lovely rock and tundra. You can't do that much now. It is against the rules. I sat by lakes and thought a lot about where I was headed. When I returned Dad's car to Sioux City he took me aside for a chat. He said, "I have been checking with the draft board here and they consider all of your training so far to be active duty. If you got out of the Navy now they would not draft you into the Army." I nodded but did not say anything. I was pretty sure from conferences with fellow cadets that other draft boards did not take a similar position.

At Preflight in Ottumwa, Iowa, I was herded into a huge gymnasium with V-5 cadets from all over the United States. It seemed like there were hundreds. An officer spoke to us, "All right, men, now is the time you sign up for four years." I was aghast. I thought the clock had been running on my enlistment period ever since they sent me to Swarthmore. You do not read the papers you sign when you enlist. At least I didn't. "If you want out, now is the time to so indicate by raising your hand," he continued. I raised my hand and so did two others. Faces turned to look at me like I was Adolph Hitler. "You, you, and you report to the captain at 0800."

When I entered the captain's office I was shaking so hard I could barely salute. He was not only the captain of the base, he was a four striper. He studied me and said, "Young man, I understand you want out of the Navy."

"Yes sir," I replied.

"Why?"

"Sir, it seems to me that you are going to have enough pilots out there to man ten navies. I am not confident of my ability for this career. I *am* confident of my skills for engineering and I know that some day I will be one. I think that I ought to get on with my education."

There was a long period of silence. The captain's eyes went down to papers on his desk, but I could tell he was not reading them. He looked up again.

"I don't blame you, son. I'd do the same thing myself if I were in your shoes."

The next day the three of us boarded a train headed toward the Great Lakes Naval Training Center. My two friends and I were billeted at a barracks in OGU, waiting for dispensation of our discharge from the armed forces. A bosun's mate approached us. He had some very unsophisticated tools in his hands and he said, "I want you three men to sweep and swab down this barracks."

"Stick it," said one of my buddies. "We're aviation cadets. We outrank you. You can't tell us what to do."

"Yeah," said the other cadet.

"Gimmee that broom," I said.

My buddies went to the brig and the next day I was a civilian.

I told my father about my brief exchange with the captain at Ottumwa. "It figures," he said. "It's usually best to deal with someone as far up the ladder as you can reach, providing you can do so gracefully." That was good advice. The top person is usually more understanding.

In order to solve any real problem which I meet as an adult, I like to think about it for a couple of days. I helped to build a business using that cautious philosophy. If I don't know the answer to a question, I think it's smart to say, "I don't know, but I'll find out." A fighter pilot has never had this option, whether he is flying an F6F *Hellcat* or an F14 *Tomcat*. The war was over and I had an opportunity to leave the Navy to continue my engineering education. The U.S. taxpayer can be thankful that I was not motivated to get my wings. I could have destroyed a lot of expensive hardware.

About twenty years after I stared with perplexity at the few dials in a Stearman cockpit, the U.S.S. *Oriskany* was steaming through the Gulf of Tonkin with freshly armed aircraft ready for an early morning strike. A fire was discovered in a locker containing magnesium flares. They began to explode on the hangar deck before a cacophony of bells and klaxons and loudspeakers could announce the problem. Crewmen struggled to move loaded planes, to jettison bombs, to direct fire hoses, and to contact trapped shipmates. Walls of the burning locker bulged with the heat and dirty grey smoke fouled the air. It poured into Officers' Country and asphyxiated twenty-four pilots. Eleven other officers and eight enlisted men died in the worst Naval disaster of the Vietnam War.

There were plenty of heroes that day on the *Oriskany,* from battle-hardened veterans to rock-and-roll teenagers. One officer, the fighter squadron exec, had to make a nasty decision, and he had to make it quickly. In order to lead blinded choking men to safety he chose to take them down through a vertical trunk into the bowels of the distressed carrier. They might drown below, but they surely would choke to death above. He directed a human chain through hatches and passageways. The men were in shock and the chain broke. He re-entered darkened voids to re-attach the chain, whose links were faulty because seared flesh would not remain intact. He made two hopeful exits to clean air without the proper number of people. A third try brought all of his desperate group to safety.

The leader who conducted these men out of a floating gas chamber was once the aspiring aviation cadet from Greeley, now a naval commander, Cal Swanson. A longer version of his name was Charles A. Lindbergh Swanson. That, friends, is motivation.

CHAPTER 11

SMOKELESS

The Grand Plan was to ride my bike into all forty-eight of the contiguous United States. The rules would be the same as those used for the passes: paved roads, leave from Lakewood, begin again from home on successive trips, rescues were O.K. So far I had ridden in eight states—Colorado, New Mexico, Wyoming, Idaho, Montana, Utah, Washington, and Oregon. It was a start.

Riding to the East Coast was a very intimidating prospect. It seemed so ghastly far. It would yield a bunch of states, but the time involvement would be incredible. I had to figure a way to split this thing up into manageable pieces. At this time, I could afford only a few days away from work, two weeks at the most. That would not get me very far. I looked at maps and decided to try a trip into the upper Midwest to states that were somewhat cut off by the Great Lakes. I would save Iowa and everything east for another time.

On Saturday, September 1, 1984, I cranked up the hill on 20th Avenue and headed toward downtown Denver from my home. In addition to the commitment for the tour, I had vowed to try something else—no cigarettes during this trip. It would be a first for me, but it would have to make things easier, I reasoned. I had given up smoking countless times before without enduring success, but I figured the physical activity of the biking would make nicotineless days and nights tolerable. I rode around Sloan's Lake down to Confluence Park and entered the Platte River bike path headed north. When the path petered out, I tried to find my way through the semi-industrial areas of northeast Denver to I-76. It didn't work. I had to ride north to Fort Lupton on U.S. 85, then east to Hudson before I could enter the interstate legally. I heard occasional gun shots. It was the opening day of dove season.

It dawned on me that I should transfer a can of beer to my left pannier, on the shady side. I stopped and zipped open the bag. Everything inside was soaked. Something had punctured the aluminum can. My sweatshirt had served as a blotter, together with rice which I carried as lightweight emergency rations. I wrung out the messy shirt and threw the rice away.

The sky ahead was black as I approached Fort Morgan. The rain kept ahead of me and I stayed dry, even though the paving was wet. I turned onto U.S. 34 and pedaled to Brush. There I pondered whether to try for Sterling. I could not measure my mileage accurately, due to false starts I had made around Commerce City, but I estimated that I had come about 104 miles. My left knee hurt and I could tell that I had not devoted the proper amount of time to break in my butt. Butts of another nature were preying on my mind. I decided to pack it in for the day and get a motel room.

This trip would turn out to be very different from those made previously in that I would seldom suffer from dehydration or the awful sapping of strength due to insufficient food intake. There were no big mountains to do me in. The weather was mostly cool. I would have other problems. Since I felt very good at first and discounted the degree of difficulty, I pushed too hard early in the trip and never quite recovered from the excess. True to my rationale about the cigarettes, I was eventually able to subdue the urge to smoke. I think, however, that I was subconsciously driving myself pitilessly.

The second day, I rode to Sterling for breakfast, a distance of about thirty-five miles. Both knees hurt during the ride, but were O.K. when I left the restaurant. I was on U.S. 6 which parallels the interstate and the South Platte River. I turned north on Highway 113. About a mile past Peetz, a wounded cock pheasant jumped out of the borrow pit on my right. He could not fly properly and fell back into the weeds. I carefully laid down the bike and went to look for him. The crafty creature eluded me. My road went east of Sidney, Nebraska, and became U.S. 385. I laughed at a sign advertising the S & M Grocery, but did not see the store as I passed through Dalton. A photo of it would have been fun. The paving north of there was brand new and it was a pleasant ride to Bridgeport, where I holed up for the night. That evening, I ordered barbecued ribs in a restaurant. They brought me the ribs, which were cold. I ate the meat off one, tried two others plus a chilly "baked" potato, then asked to have the food reheated. Next they brought my bowl of soup, then a salad with no dressing. Later, they brought in a brand new plate of ribs. The potato was hot. The ribs were still cold.

The next morning, I decided to try the other restaurant. It took forty minutes to receive two eggs. I stayed on 385 and crossed the North Platte River. A head wind blasted me as I came off a plateau south of Alliance. There I was detoured northwest onto Highway 2. The detour went due north at Berea, but it was gravel. I continued on the paving to Hemingford, had lunch and rode north near the Box Butte Dam on the Niobrara River. Some people were tubing on the tiny stream. I stopped in the shade to relax and enjoy them. The day was now extremely hot and I had not taken any precautions against the sun. I was getting badly burned. My left knee and sore rear troubled me as I rode east, then north over many hills into Chadron. I stopped at a liquor store to buy a cold can of beer and call Arch's brother. Manny, Sheila, and Felicia Archuleta entertained me at their home that evening. Manny tempted me with more beer and then asked, "Do you like barbecued ribs?" I told him they were one of my favorites. They were delicious.

From Chadron, I headed north through Hot Springs and up tough hills to Custer, where I spent the night. During my lunch break that day, I had leaned my bike and my body against a sign in Wind Cave National Park. A huge buffalo sneaked up behind me to say howdie. When I finally heard and then saw him, I almost jumped out of my socks. The next day, I climbed a long grade and passed the entry to Crazy Horse Monument with mixed emotions about the carving of our wilderness to create a tourist trap. Then I cranked through the Black Hills until I saw autos of tourists parked forward of me with people staring up over my head. I stopped to look back. The presidential heads loomed above a ridge in the sunshine. It was a very moving sight. I inspected the obligatory artifacts at the Memorial Headquarters, none of which compared to my first view of the carved stone heads above the trees.

I hurried through Rapid City and turned onto I-90. The traffic got fierce and the shoulder was very rough. There was no riding where it was "safe" and the car drivers could not comprehend this. They were really perturbed with me. Near Ellsworth Air Force Base, a funeral procession passed me. Not wishing to make it a double, I quit for the day at New Underwood, staying at "Jake's New Motel" which was very clean and cozy.

On my sixth day out, I turned off the interstate at Wall after a visit to the famed drug store. I headed south toward the Badlands. It was a real struggle getting to the national park entrance because of a west-southwest wind. I stopped to photograph some horses with their manes blowing in the air. The picture turned out to be a beauty. As the road curled east I was blown through the exotic terrain. This is a classic bike ride, one well suited for even a novice. The loop south from I-90 through the Badlands provides a picturesque and easy forty-mile ride. Try to take the direction best suited to the wind conditions, which in South Dakota can be very capricious. I stopped for the night in Belvidere. The motel operator, Bret, gave me a cold can of beer. I walked my bike to the room and was followed by three little boys about seven or eight years old. They had their own bicycles, fat-tired and filthy. The boys asked if they could come in to see my bike, I said, "Sure," so they dropped their bikes and charged into the room. Their caboose was a little girl about four. She was a doll. I watched them appraise my equipment in the crowded space.

"What are those things?" one asked.

"Those are gear shifters."

"What are they for?"

"They help me go up steep hills."

"How?"

"My legs can go faster and I don't get as tired." This didn't make any sense. My stock went down about ten points.

"Why are the handlebars bent funny?"

"So I can ride long distances in a comfortable position and get out of the wind." I could tell they weren't buying it. I lost another ten points.

"Did you come far?"

"Very far."

"As far as Rapid City?"

"Farther than Rapid City."

"Wow!" I gained back maybe five.

"Why don't you have fenders? Our bikes have fenders."

"I can see that. Maybe I should get some." There went the five point gain.

"What's this stuff?"

"That's a tent, sleeping bag, and pad."

"Why do you need that if you sleep here?"

"Sometimes I can't find a nice place like this and I have to camp out." Down five more.

"Wanna go for a ride with us?"

"That's very nice of you to invite me, but I don't think so. I'm very tired and I have to take a shower." They filed out, picked up their bikes and rode off, popping wheelies. The little girl ran behind. I sighed and opened the beer. "Face it, Bob," I thought, "it's Chapter 11. You sure didn't impress those little guys." I was thankful not to have suffered the ultimate humiliation. I can't do a wheelie.

That night, Marguerite, the bartender in town, and Kay, who kept the restaurant open for me, both treated me very well. Their questions were not as penetrating.

I took the service road east, which was a mistake. It was hillier and rougher than the interstate. I had wanted to go northward through Hayes but learned that the road through there was under construction. It was imperative that I turn soon in order to make my way into North Dakota, but the wind was out of the west and I enjoyed the help. Just short of Okaton, the shift cable to my rear derailleur broke. But hey, no problem, you can't catch ol' Bob twice with the same dilemma. I now carried a spare for just such an emergency. Good thinking, right? Wrong. I had nothing with me to cut a nub off one end of the cable and could not, therefore, thread it through the housings. I found a rock shop where the owner laid my cable on his vise and cut it with a cold chisel.

At Vivian, I turned north into the Fort Pierre National Grasslands. Riding now was very inefficient because of the crosswind. At a bike shop in Pierre I purchased another cable and asked a young man to cut the nub off one end. I also asked him to look at my chain because it was loose and dirty and I was throwing it off the cogs every so often, jamming it into the frame. He estimated a useful life for the chain of about ten more miles. I didn't buy a new one because I hated to put it on my grungy gears and I was anxious to get on the road to take advantage of the strong west wind. The wind betrayed me at Harrold. I set up camp there in a miniature park. Some kids threw rocks at my tent and I waited impatiently for darkness and their bedtime. I figured the day's effort to have yielded 113 miles.

The next night I was in Clark. I had covered 127 more miles but I was very depressed. I could rocket pretty well going east, but any turn north caused an unstable posture leaning into the crosswind. If a truck passed, I had to be on guard completely to avoid turning into it as I was momentarily shielded. I had entered U.S. 212 at Redfield after riding around Cottonwood Lake. I was throwing the chain again which is only fun if you have a grease fetish. Highway 212 is the road described by Barbara Savage in her fine book *Miles From Nowhere*. She did not care much for 212 or South Dakota. For her and her companion it was a boring, hot, mosquito-filled, windy, painful ride. There is a color photo of 212 in her book, showing the endless stretch of road progressing through the grasslands. I didn't find this environment boring. It was beautiful. But I like *big* country. It is a great challenge to a biker.

I did not suffer from heat or mosquitoes. Nor did I encounter endless headwind in South Dakota. I've had my share in other states. Riding into a gale for hours on end can work fiercely on your mind. You begin to think that the wind will *never* let up. Riding up a pass can be equally punishing, but you know the agony will end. I was very blue and hurty that night, but in retrospect it was my own fault. I had blown out my knees early and they would never recover until I eased back on the mileage. I wrote in my log that touring was a dumb jock egomaniac selfish enterprise.

I felt so bad that I was ready to quit. I called Anne. It was Saturday.

"I'm having some problems here. When can you leave?"

"I can't start until Monday and I don't want to drive to Sioux City in one day. I should also spend some time there with mother."

"Well, so be it. I'll call you at her place Tuesday evening."

"Have you any idea where you will be then?"

"I haven't the foggiest. I'm having a very difficult time getting the bike up into North Dakota. The wind is awful and my chain is shot and my rear is sore and my knees hurt and . . ."

When I next talked to Anne, it was from a miserable motel in Long Lake, Minnesota. It was raining and I had no idea where I could get some dinner and I had very little food. I had somehow managed to get through the winds into North Dakota, just catching the corner of the state at Fairmount before turning into Minnesota and then southeast on Highway 9. At one point, receiving good advice from a friendly motorist, I carried the bike across a wooden railroad bridge to avoid a twenty-mile detour.

"Where are you?" Anne asked.

"I'm in a suburb just west of Minneapolis." I looked at the map. "Can you meet me in Northfield? It's south of the Twin Cities. That should give you an easy day of driving."

"Yes. I'll try."

"Good. If I haven't left a note at the post office, then I will still be out on the road. You don't need to hurry. I Want to ride into

Wisconsin and back. You might look for me on Highway 47. Can you find it on the map?"

"Yes I see it. What's the weather like?"

"It's pouring rain now. I hope it gets better by morning."

It was still raining at dawn, but not as hard. I didn't have any choice but to get on the bike and go. If I got soaked, it would be difficult to hole up somewhere, because I did not have a way of contacting Anne in Northfield. We would have to "find" each other by telephoning her mother in Sioux City.

Highway 12 became Wayzata Boulevard. I was terrified. The early morning traffic was awful. I was particularly wary when crossing entry and exit ramps. Cars whizzed by and splashed me. I had on my orange Goretex rain jacket, more for visibility than to keep dry. Nearing the downtown area, I was directed off the freeway by a sign. I had to stand still for ten minutes before an opening in the traffic allowed me to walk across to a down ramp. Among the big buildings, I was lost. A helpful service station attendant directed me to Highway 55. At Hastings, I crossed the Mississippi River and then realized that I would have to ride east across the St. Croix River to get into Wisconsin. A lift bridge raised just after I entered Prescott. Since I was momentarily trapped there, I rode out of town for about a mile before heading back.

To say that I biked Wisconsin would be laughable. But I did get the Chinese Thunderbird just into the state, from Lakewood, Colorado. I ate lunch back in Hastings and found Highway 47. The humidity was high and I sweat heavily, cranking hard for Northfield. It was a delight to see the black Saab coming at me, horn blaring. Anne and I kissed and she handed me a beer. We laughed and talked and I loaded my gear into the car. I was so pumped up that I forgot to check the mileage into town. It was probably about fifteen. Anne giggled at me because I drove so slowly. It took strong concentration and bravery to go over 35 mph.

We found a delightful old hotel, which had just been redecorated. We were told to walk through all the rooms (with a tour guide and price list in hand) before selecting our suite. We chose one of the less expensive accommodations. It was about three times more costly than anything I had been in for a long while, but what the hell. That night we had a fine dinner and I remained tobacco free even though Anne smoked her normal quota of cigarettes.

I had chosen Northfield because it was the site of the last job by the James and Younger gang. Someone tipped off the populace about their holdup, so folks ambushed them at the bank. The bank is now a museum. It contains life-size photos of the dead bodies of the would-be robbers. The pictures are what my daughters would refer to as gross, complete with bullet holes and vacant stares. I mailed copies on post cards to my office, claiming that they represented my condition at the end of the tour. No one thought this was funny.

Anne took a picture of my hands up against the wall of the bank. It looked like I had a mild case of leprosy. The sun had burned the distinctive biker's glove pattern into my skin, many tiny spots and one circle on the back of each hand. We got in the car and toured the campus of St. Olaf College and Carlton College.

Anne and I had a very pleasant drive home, stopping in Sioux City to again visit with her mother and spend the night. I remained tough and pure, abstaining from cigarettes all through the 1,217-mile bike ride, the drive home in the car, and my subsequent return to work. Two weeks later, I had a heart attack.

CHAPTER 12

DECISIONS

It was a terrible morning. I was driving to a business meeting and heard Dick Gibson announce on KADX that Shelly Manne had died the day before. Stan Kenton had died in 1979, on my birthday, and now Shelly was gone. The great jazz artists whom I admired so much were dropping like flies.

I talked to Shelly briefly once when he gave a little seminar at Wheat Ridge High School. He and I both showed up one hour early due to an incorrect program notice. We were the only people in the auditorium, so I decided to introduce myself.

"I first heard you play with Kenton in a field house at Iowa State College. That would have been 1946 or thereabouts," I said.

"Wow, that was a long time ago. *You* must be ancient." We both laughed.

I was probably the only non-drummer in his audience at Wheat Ridge. Shelly mostly talked that day. When he did play, it was to make a point.

"You can have all the great moves and gorgeous athletic solos in the world, but unless you can do this, you are nowhere," he said. Then he picked up one stick and began to attack a single cymbal with a driving rhythmic beat. That is all he did—one hand—no drums. It brought appreciative applause. "Your primary obligation is to move the band, not be an all-star." I picked up on this because a strong team effort has always turned me on.

The sad news about Shelly did not enhance my attitude for the meeting I was approaching. Our client's client had once again changed his mind. All of the design team, working on a fixed fee, were expected to just grin and bear it, incorporating changes to the design and documents already prepared without any additional compensation. It was happening too often lately, and I was becoming very cynical about certain practices of our clientele. How could sophisticated owners and developers expect their consultant to turn cartwheels for nothing? Or was it that attitude which now made them "sophisticated"?

The meeting went about as I had anticipated. We were hammered. I drove home for lunch and the minute I walked through the door Anne knew something was wrong. My face has always telegraphed my feelings. She questioned me. "I'm sad and I'm mad," I said, and I explained why on both counts. I returned to the office at precisely 1:00 P.M. At 1:05 I was in trouble.

The symptoms were classic. I was pretty sure what was happening. I was nauseated, breaking out in a sweat, my arms and hands hurt like hell, and there was a big elephant sitting on my chest. I squatted down on the floor, took some deep breaths and tried to shake it off. One of my people could see my antics through the window to my private office. He came to the door and said, "What's the problem, Bob?"

"I think I'm having a heart attack."

"You'd better get to a hospital. I'll drive you."

"I suppose you're right, but I can drive myself."

We argued and I won. I drove myself to the hospital. This was totally dumb, but I was embarrassed. I drove way too fast and ran two red lights. When I announced what was happening at the emergency room, the technicians went into action in a hurry. Then I got embarrassed again.

"It's probably indigestion," I offered. "I had some hot cheese for lunch."

"Sure. You just relax and lie right there. We'll know tomorrow if it's indigestion. We have a nifty little enzyme test that reveals all."

"Tomorrow? You mean I have to stay here?"

"We will be moving you up to coronary care in a few minutes."

In my new bed in C.C.U., I was wired up to all kinds of equipment and told by a tough nurse how to perform. I lay there and contemplated my predicament. Later on I was convinced that the enzyme test was a waste of time, because I had another jolt. It wasn't particularly painful, just weighty. I breathed deeply and lay still, kind of checking it out. The nurse ran in and chewed on me. "Don't do that," she said. "You're supposed to hit the button."

A cardiologist was assigned to me. We never got along very well. He never said very much and what he did say I could not understand. I was told that they wanted to do an angiogram on me but that meant changing hospitals. They made it sound like a little nuisance sort of thing. I was admitted at the second hospital and handed a form to read and sign. It was a release. Apparently the angiogram involved some risk, but I was too chicken not to sign. Hey, did that procedure turn out to be a lot of fun! They shove a coat hanger into a blood vessel in your groin and try to make it travel to your heart. They start that far away from the target so it can be like a game. If the wire comes out your ear they can all have a good laugh and start over. I had a misconception that this would be a very delicate precise process, involving meticulous movements. The cardiologist was going through motions like he was fly casting. You get to see this hollow wire enter your heart on a TV screen hanging overhead. I would rather have watched a soap. They pump some ink through the wire so they can tell if your heart is still working. It makes nice designs on the monitor. The ink causes hot flashes and you get one gigantic surge akin to the possible pollution from pulling out of a 9G dive. Then they remove the wire. I was full of blood thinner and the hole in my leg would not clot. A nurse had to stand over me for about thirty minutes, pressing down with both of her hands on my thigh. There were some benefits.

They were trying to decide what to do with me. When Anne and I queried the cardiologist, he said that on paper I looked good. I didn't want to look good on paper. I wanted to live. He didn't think surgery was warranted. That was good news. They released me from the hospital. I didn't see that a whole lot had been accomplished other than scaring me half to death. My insurance company had to cough up about eight thousand dollars.

The big problem with surviving a heart attack (and the opposite scenario has absolutely no redeeming qualities) is what it does to your head. All of a sudden, you become aware of your mortality. I suppose that isn't all bad. Everyone tells you to live each day one at a time. I didn't know there were other choices. The doctors and nurses were amazed that I had quit smoking and ridden a bike for twelve hundred miles two weeks before my hospitalization. I wasn't. I enrolled in a cardiac rehabilitation program and every time I crawled onto one of their exercise bikes, I would almost burn it up. Someone would come over and shut me down. Activity of a physical nature wasn't the problem. I now think that I almost did myself in with my own hostility. The big rides on the bike probably saved me from an early demise. The Destroyer? What an inappropriate name I had assigned to Anne's gift.

I still had chest pains and I was depressed. Anxiety over one's health can be a real downer. Most of the medical professionals are too wary to be uplifting. Your family and friends try to be supportive, but it has to come from within. I told Jo Skinner about my problems and she mentioned them to a cardiologist whom she knew quite well. He went over to look at the movies of my heart, called her back, and told her to have me call him immediately. He said that I needed surgery—RIGHT NOW. This put me in a panic. He made photocopies of a technical treatise on aneurisms and handed them to me. I went to the family doctor and asked his advice, "I'm getting conflicting opinions. Who would you believe?"

"You need a referee, a third opinion." He wasn't about to state his own opinion. I think he discounted my whole heart attack episode as ever really happening.

"Who would you recommend?"

"Well, you have two cardiologists at odds. I'd recommend a surgeon. I know a very good one." A surgeon! Holy moly. I could just imagine what he would say.

It was a premier gala, for me, the surgeon, a radiologist, and the new cardiologist. They all stared at the moving picture of my pump. I tried to watch impassively, but it was difficult. We looked at the whorls and eddies in my tiny rivers. They backed up the film and we watched again. They muttered to each other, things I could not comprehend. Then the surgeon turned to the cardiologist and said, "I suppose we could do a bypass on this gentleman, but what are we going to achieve? I think it's a waste of time. The surgery itself isn't without risk, you know." There were two ways for me to take this. I chose the most positive, then considered licking the surgeon's hand but rejected that in favor of a warm smile.

The hurts persisted. The discomfort in my chest disturbed me more from the mental aspect than physical. The cardiologist ran a battery of new tests on me. He finally announced, "I don't know what is smarting in your chest, but it isn't angina." The family doctor arranged for x-rays to be made after I downed spooky liquids. The results were sent to a gastroenterologist for interpretation. He was very thorough, very friendly, and HE COULD COMMUNICATE. I spent over an hour writing answers to a medical survey. He talked to me for another hour, first questions and then a statement.

"You have a gallstone. It's what we call a "silent" gallstone. You have had it for years and it will probably never bother you. You also have a small hiatal hernia. I don't think it's a problem. You don't have angina, that's for sure. What I think you are suffering from is depression. You certainly have every reason to be debilitated by this malady, which can have nasty physical effects. It is as real as any other sickness. I know that you have a strong dislike for drugs, but I wish you would consider trying one which we prescribe for this problem. The results could surprise you."

It turned out that this specialist identified the problem. It is strange that the only doctors I could ever talk with, he and my family physician, have the same last name though they are unrelated. Why is it that so many doctors are poor at communicating with their patients? It isn't believable any more that they are godlike. I saw a woman on Nova who I would like to have as my doctor. It isn't likely. Her name is Susan M. Love and she does breast surgery for cancer. From her remarks it is obvious that she understands the importance of communication, particularly when medical knowledge is incomplete and the options are not clear cut. Dammit, if you don't know, say so. I can live with that. I can also die with it. I have news for you. I don't think anyone is going to leave this place alive.

I thought about the depression medicine for a few days, and then we tried one. Despite some strange and wonderful side effects, a gradual increase in dosage made the world tolerable again. I was able to get my act together.

Bud and I opened a tiny structural engineering office in 1956. It was a no-frills operation. Bob Hoefer, a high school friend from Sioux City, searched out our office and said, "I knew I was getting close when I saw all the junkyards." Our monthly rent for office space was forty-five dollars. We did anything that was honest and even remotely connected to engineering to make a buck. We had the idea that, "You build a better mousetrap, and . . ." It worked for a long time. The business thrived, and it was really fun to work hard.

Bud was better than a genius. He *was* very smart, but best of all, he was practical. He and I complemented each other. He was easy going and laid back. I was a meticulous worry wart. We attracted different types of clients. Bud was very creative and imaginative. I never had an original idea in my life, but I could improve things. Bud was the finest engineer I ever worked with, and I have worked with many.

When Arch became the third manager of the firm, we added a new dimension, a younger and enthusiastic leader who filled some gaps. He had instant insight to any problem and he was seldom wrong.

As our work load and staff increased, we did some very innovative things. We designed the first structural steel folded plate, the first timber folded plate, the first true space frame in Colorado. Until superseded by another firm's effort, we designed the world's longest prestressed concrete girder and a support system for the largest array of solar collectors. We had, I think, the trust of our clients and the respect of our competitors. We won some awards, but the most treasured accolade in my view was an occasional compliment from a construction worker or fabricator who appreciated a novel solution.

We did some things that I would not attempt today. I wouldn't take the chance now because of the propensity for people to sue. It colors your thinking. I used to have the naive concept that a professional could never be held liable for a mistake as long as he had not been negligent in performing his duty. How can a person be punished just for making a mistake? To err is human, and all that. Now, it seems that no one can tolerate any sort of risk. There must be recompense for any fault or error. Someone must pay. Sure, but always someone else?

It got to be no fun looking over my shoulder. Had I screwed up? Had an employee screwed up? The penalty could be severe. Even with an error-free record of performance, the cost of doing business increased dramatically every year due to the dollars spent on insurance.

Then we started to have other problems. Many people in the building fields did not know what they were doing. Thinly financed owners and developers (you know some of their names) sought instant solutions from architects and engineers. Competition to acquire projects got fiercer. Construction costs were "saved" up front with inadequate design fees. Some designers and builders were no longer masters of their craft. They became hustlers and brokers. Previously loyal clients asked us to bid on projects, for the right to design a faultless yet still economical structure.

All the while, everyone tried to impress everyone else with how good they were at what they did. This was called "marketing." Everyone was so busy advertising that they almost forgot to do anything or make anything. I grieved for a nation burying itself in its own hype. I don't think I was bitter, just sad. I have great respect for anyone who can *do* something, even if it's carving a straighter side on a ditch. Doesn't anyone like to work anymore? I *was* angry, mostly at myself because I couldn't cope well with the new rules: lawsuits, incompetence, disloyalty, marketing. I had made the transition from slide rules to calculators to computers. New products and design techniques did not bother me. If I could not manage these tools, there were plenty of younger people in our firm who were quite capable. It was the change in humanistic values which upset me—the work ethic. How dare they change the rules during my lifetime.

When the walkways collapsed at the tea dance in the Hyatt Regency in Kansas City, I came to consider the failure as a signal of the end. Structural engineering, for me at least, would never be quite the same. I was asked by one team of experts to help with studies and testimony on the tragedy in Missouri. I was very happy to decline on the grounds that I was acquainted with one of the engineers.

In early 1986, I resigned from the company I helped to found. By then, we had designed over five thousand projects. Bud and Arch were long gone, they got discouraged with the whole scene earlier than I. As an engineer, I'm supposed to be very logical. I made a list, pros and cons on leaving versus staying. Then I made a discovery. I found another list in my desk. It was five years old and itemized the same things. It was time to make an emotional, not necessarily logical, decision. It was time to leave.

Since my exit from a structural engineering firm, I have done a number of different things, some of them pretty goofy. I did not intend to retire. I have suffered through two sales jobs, driven as a courier, done contract painting, served as census taker and commercial arbitrator, delivered expert testimony, "performed" as a TV extra, managed property and investments, completed some volunteer tasks, written a book, and toured on the bike. You could not say I lacked employment. I wonder what is next.

CHAPTER 13

TO THE BEACH

I called Arch as soon as I saw the article in the paper. "There's some verbiage in the business section of the *Post* about your company," I said. "It isn't very complimentary. I thought I should call because I know that no one up there reads a Denver paper. Actually, I wasn't sure whether any of you could read." Arch is a director of Boulder Beer.

"What does it say?"

"It tells how the company is losing money."

"There isn't a brewery in the world that makes a profit at first. It will take a few years."

"In the meantime, you could use some good press. Why doesn't Boulder Beer sponsor me for a bike ride to the East Coast? You market in Nebraska and all over New England. I could wear your weird T-shirts and your reps could take my picture on the bike and do with it what they will. A good writer could get a lot of advertising mileage out of my trip."

"Bob, that's probably the best idea you ever had. In fact, it's probably the only idea you ever had. I'll call Jerry Smart and tell him what you just said."

"Who's he?"

"Jerry is president of the company."

I received a phone call from Jerry in less than an hour. He was ecstatic.

"This is a great concept. Our people here can do a lot with this and so can our distributors back east. We'll get you on the 'Tonight Show.'" His last remark made me uneasy.

"I have a couple of provisos that you should be aware of," I said.

"What are they?"

"I had a heart attack some time ago, so I don't want to deal with the stress of trying to arrive at a specific location at a prearranged time. It's very difficult on a bicycle. Also, I will need some financial help. I don't want to camp out much on a heavy-duty trip like this. I will have motel and restaurant expenses, plus I need air fare back."

"I understand. We won't put any heat on you timewise. Any pressure of that sort will be your own doing. Figure out what your costs will be and let me know."

When I first caught this brain wave it appeared to be a method to finance my tour east and gather a few dollars more. Subsequent conversations with Arch alerted me to the fact that their brewery was struggling and that this idea of mine could be no bonanza. Nevertheless, I was excited about the prospect and started to ride little jaunts to prepare my body. I agonized over what to tell Jerry before I finally called him. "I'll do it for the flat sum of twelve hundred dollars. I hope I can pay for most of my costs with that."

"Oh, well, yeah, O.K. Uh, let me go over this with our people and I will get back with you." I knew that I had blown it. He called back to say that an expense of that amount was more than their budget could tolerate right then. I was very disappointed because I was all psyched up for a trip and had committed time for it and forced myself to get in shape. I didn't think I could afford to foot the bills for a trip east, but I wanted to go somewhere. I decided to go west.

Bud and Arch and I were having lunch in Boulder. "You are going to fry out there," Bud said. "There is *nothing* south of St. George."

"The plan is for Anne to sag me through the desert," I said. "She can rescue me if the heat gets too fierce. Besides, I'm leaving fairly early in the spring. Temperatures aren't at their max yet. I have to do it sometime. I have to get Arizona, Nevada, and California." Bud just looked at me. I'm sure that he thought I had slipped a cog. I had become a state bagger.

"It's just another death ride," said Arch.

The people were so nice. A motorist stopped me just east of Dillon. He pulled his van over and waited to see if I needed a place to stay. Near the west end of Glenwood Canyon, Mary Lou helped me lift my heavy bike into her truck which was the lead vehicle of a caravan through the highway construction. A voice on her radio embarrassed both of us, "Mary Lou, you sure will go to great lengths to pick up a man." Waitresses in Rifle and at Rosie's Restaurant in Palisade were very solicitous.

I reached Fruita in three days. The grind over Loveland Pass had been a bear, as always. This was my third attack at Loveland. I had ridden some of it once with the Crazies, but that "didn't count" because I hadn't started from Lakewood. The ride from Frisco to Copper Mountain hurt more than the haul over Vail Pass. I have no idea why. I was saying a little prayer before I got on the bike each morning. It was only a year and a half since my heart problems and I did not know what my body could tolerate. I had ridden in New Mexico with the Crazies during the spring of '85, but I had taken it very easy on that trip. While I was riding now I was experiencing peculiar sensations like my brain was fried, tiny twinges of hurt in my head, sharp and quick. They worried me. Was I an accident looking for a place to happen? I couldn't get any health insurance which was worth much. My bad "history" would not allow it. Major medical coverage excluded any heart-related problems. It did not matter to anyone that I could crank a bike over an awesome pass. Were the insurance companies correct? Was I an inordinate risk? Was the discomfort in my head put there to tell me something?

The little head hurts quit after two days. One of the beauties of a long bike tour is that you can't dwell on anything sad for very long. Too many things are happening. A lot of them are fun. Dealing with the logistics of the trip requires concentration. People say to me, "Don't you get bored?" They must think of me as performing like an automaton in a vacuum, downstroking through a thoughtless void. That's the exercise bicycle syndrome, what you get astride that dumb machine in your basement. It doesn't happen out here.

I heard once about a swell technique for worrying. You select a special hour of each day and just worry like hell over everything you can think of. I tried it on a tour. It did not work. My mind kept wandering to happy thoughts.

Getting to Green River, Utah, was a chore. It was the wind, not the grade. I crept along the highway with only one gear combination in reserve. The next day, my route took me off I-70 onto Highway 24 toward Hanksville. Adjacent to the Goblin Valley State Park was a long fun downgrade. I pedaled to Capitol Reef National park, where I was told that the campgrounds were full. I decided to chance them anyway and ask someone if I could share their space. I was a little wary, because I was attired in the shiny red biking shorts which Anne purchased for me. People stare a lot at those pants. They would be considered revealing if you had anything to reveal. Woody avoids me when I wear them. In New Mexico he said, "You go in the restaurant first. If you don't get thrown out or into a fight, then we'll come in." I found a couple who ignored my shorts and said I could use part of their space. They were sitting on a blanket reading the Bible to each other. I set up my tent but had to move it under a tree. It got too hot in the sunlight. I hid in the tent and drank vodka and nursed sunburned ankles. My ultra-short socks offered no protection to the white skin and, like always, I had neglected to grease up. I wrote in my notes, "What is the matter with me? I haven't learned a thing in six years."

The following day, I believed that I had discovered the worst roads in the United States. In the early A.M. as I rode through the park, I thought my bike was broken. It would hardly move. I stopped to look it over carefully. Then I looked back down the highway I had covered. It was a deceptively steep grade, probably eight percent or more. No wonder the bike would not move. The road got worse. It was cracked, bumpy, and had little or no shoulder. Portions were chip-sealed with small rocks which presented a rough and hazardous ride. West of Loa, Utah, was a mean hill which eventually led to a summit of about 8,350 feet. Then there was a quick descent and a turn south on Highway 62. The drop into a valley produced instant heat. I heard a sound like a pack of dogs chewing on peanut butter. I looked down. My legs were covered with tar. Asphalt was bleeding up through sand covering cracks in the roadway. The glop was ravelling off the sidewalls of my tires and jamming in the brake pads. The bike came to a stop. I searched for a stick to clean the goo from the bicycle so the wheels would rotate. The road patching had obviously been made with faulty materials which melted at too low a temperature. I had to thread my way through a maze of tarry rivers and stop every so often to clean debris from the bike. The first thing I did when I pulled into Circleville was search for a store where I could buy a can of mineral spirits. I didn't need a gallon, but that was the only size available.

I could not start riding until 9:30 the following morning because it took until then to take the bicycle apart and clean it. The motel owner had donated a pile of rags. I was told by the natives that it was downhill all the way to St. George. They would make poor civil engineers because this was not quite true. People who just drive automobiles are not totally conscious of the terrain around them. They may have some feel for the country, but they are not aware of or concerned about hills like a cyclist is. I have quit asking people about the hills "up ahead." Their predictions are not always accurate. If you want an overview of the slope of the land, it's best to observe which way the streams flow.

In the evening, I got a room in a tiny motel about one mile north of Mt. Carmel Junction. I was forced to backtrack because everything else was full. It was Sunday on Memorial Day weekend. I had passed on the opportunity to visit Bryce Canyon National Park. The road would have taken me out of my way on a tough climb during the heat of the day and the holiday traffic made overnight facilities very tenuous. I had been on the road exactly one week and was averaging about ninety miles a day.

At the entrance to Zion National Park, a lady asked me my intent. When I told her that I was headed straight through, she said that a ranger would meet me at the east end of the tunnel in about forty-five minutes. I lollygagged down the road, stopping to take photos and talk to bikers going the other way. The rock formations were marvelous.

The tunnel is long, it's dark, and the road turns. It is spooky riding through with a ranger following in a truck to light the way. I would have liked to stop to look out the windows into the valley to the north, but had been told to keep moving. It was even spookier dropping down to the valley on a switchbacked roadway. They had sanded the paving with loose purple aggregate. Sand is the bane of a biker; it is so easy to fall with the slightest turn. I was thankful not to be heading upgrade like the riders I passed, but the heat lower down in the valley was awful. I could feel the moisture being sucked out of my body. It had snowed on Loveland Pass. Now I was in an oven. On the west side of Hurricane, I pulled into a service station to get water. I drank all I could, filled my bottles, and then saw that my rear tire was flat. There was a glass fragment in the casing. I was fortunate to have shade to work in because I totally botched the first two repair efforts. I left the service station feeling like an inept idiot.

Interstate 15 was only ten miles ahead. It was a great sweating effort just to get there. I hid in the shade of an overpass before entering the freeway, eating fruit and drinking water. The water in my bottles was hot. Returning weekend traffic crowded the interstate. The temperature was 105 degrees when I reached St. George. A lady was passing through the lobby of the motel as I registered. She looked at me and stopped.

"What have you done to your ankle?" she asked.

"It's just sunburn." I looked down. It was a blistered mess.

"That could get infected. I am a nurse. Let me bring you something." She brought a tube of Silvadene to my room and told me to keep it. I showered and applied the silver salve.

I called Anne. "This isn't going to work," I said. "You would fry down here sitting in that black car waiting for me to move down the highway. Don't even think about driving out here."

"What are you going to do, then?"

"I will start as early in the mornings as possible. I will be very careful to make sure that I can get out of the heat."

Then the trek through the desert began. My mileage went way down. I would get on the road each day at first light. The truckers could not see me well at the early hour, but I had a super wide shoulder on which to ride. As the light increased, the trucks pulled out to give me a wide berth if they could change lanes safely. The over-the-road truckers, at least in the West, are very courteous to me. I have never confirmed this with a serious study, but it seems to me that the drivers of big trucks have a certain rapport with loaded bicycle tourers. We have common problems. We both have to deal with the wind. We both have to go through the gears.

I rode to Glendale, quit before noon and registered at a motel. I had ridden seventy miles. I bought a six pack of beer and stared at the tube. I thought about the beautiful ride into Arizona through the Virgin River Gorge. Arizonans won't like me. I didn't do justice to their state. I only caught a corner.

The next day I was confused in Las Vegas when signs directed me to leave the interstate. I muddled my way through the city and pushed on to the newly opened Whiskey Pete's, right on the Nevada-California state line, quitting at 1:15 P.M. after ninety-two sweat-soaked miles. The casinos on the Nevada border were a boon, because food was superlative and inexpensive.

The road into California was flat for about six miles, then offered a tough granny crank for about ten miles, descended into a basin with a rest stop and climbed gradually west. There was a fine downhill roll of about fifteen miles into Baker. It was 9:30 in the morning and I had covered fifty miles. Big deal. Not much for one day. Should I try for Barstow? Discretion was the better part of valor. I got a motel room with a TV and bought a small bottle of vodka. The motel had a pool but it did not interest me. It was too hot to be outside.

It was a good thing I quit at Baker. The next day I barely survived the ride to Barstow. I suffered with the heat and the wind. Signage forced me off the interstate about eight miles from town. An alternate route was not indicated. I rode a few miles south towards Daggett, then west parallel to some railroad tracks. There was no choice but to enter I-40. This was ridiculous. I complimented California on its astute planning, to force me off one interstate onto another. I struggled into Barstow at noon, totally dehydrated and weak from insufficient food and water. It was cloudy when I stepped out of my cool motel room to go for a walk that evening, but the heat was a suffocating blanket.

I left Barstow in the dark at 5:15 A.M. A moderate headwind increased in velocity as I rode southwest. I cranked a small pass and rode toward Victorville. Just short of the town, a highway patrolman streaked by. "Get that thing off the highway," he shouted at me through a loudspeaker. Then I saw him stop a truck at an exit ahead, so I pulled alongside and peered into his car.

"What's the problem?" I asked.

"You can't ride on an interstate in California. Take this ramp and get off."

"You're wrong, sir. I've ridden all the way from Denver and I wouldn't be here if I hadn't checked this out. There is hardly any other way to get into California except on interstates. How do you explain the signs on them near the towns which say 'Bicycles Exit Here'?"

"I don't give a damn. You're not riding my section of highway."

"Where do you expect me to ride?"

"What's your destination?"

"Huntington Beach."

"You'll have to go over to Palmdale." I looked at my map to try to find Palmdale. It was over forty miles west.

"That's ridiculous," I said. I was so steamed that I could not think, neglecting to record his name or number. I took the exit and went into town to inquire about an alternate route south. Palmdale was out of my way and it looked like I would still have to ride freeways from there, too. No one could assure me of a bike route to Los Angeles, but they told me how to get to Hesperia. There I asked more questions. I was directed east and south on Silverwood Lake Road. I pedaled hard, cursing the cop for every extra mile, then flagged another biker coming toward me, told him what had happened and what I was trying to do.

"The guy is a jerk," he said. "Just stay on 138. You will top a little ridge and then have to get on I-15 again at Cajon Junction. The signs will tell you when to exit as you approach L.A."

"What if I run into the patrolman again?"

"You probably won't come in contact with him. Besides, what other choice do you have?"

I had to walk the bike over the last pitch on the "little ridge" he told me about. It was too steep to manage. Everything else was just as he described it. I wandered west through the suburbs of Los Angeles on Summit Avenue, Highland Avenue, and Foothill Boulevard. I saw some kids washing cars at a church. It was a youth outing to make a few bucks. I was very hot and sweaty. "Can you wash me?" I asked.

"You mean bike and all?"

"No, just me." They loved it, blasting me with a hose. I loved it, too.

I had a flat in Azusa, caused by a staple. I called Doug Watland to warn him of my approach and ask how far it was.

"It's only about twenty miles," he said. It seemed like forty. Actually, I suppose it was something in between. I found Highway 39, which took me through Hacienda Heights to La Habra Heights. I did not need the diversion of this little climb at a late hour when my strength was fading. The traffic was heavy, but I felt comfortable with the sensation that drivers here were very biker conscious. No one gave my outrageous equipment anything more than a glance, but they seemed to be very aware of my presence. The light was fading, but I could only proceed at a given pace due to the succession of traffic signals on Beach Boulevard. I wasn't too sure of my surroundings. I knew that if I passed a big storage tank and could see the ocean, then I was in the vicinity of Doug's house. Doug flagged me down in the dark. He led me to his home about a mile away. It had been a huge grueling day, about 145 miles, no thanks to the patrolman.

Doug and Mary entertained me for a few days while I waited to board a plane. I went on some excursions of my own. I rode my bike, empty, down to Newport Beach to lust after the boats, then went to see where Stan Kenton really started to cook at the Rendezvous Ballroom in Balboa. I remembered first hearing the throaty reeds and dazzling brass of his band playing groovy chords over national airwaves in the summer of 1941. The sound was so great then that I knew the band would make it, even at my tender age.

Since I was into the nostalgia thing, Doug and Mary drove me down to San Diego. We had a fine luncheon in Old Town and then searched for the junior high school which I had attended for two years and the apartment where I had lived as a little boy. They were still in evidence on the northeast edge of Balboa Park. We watched people perform on trick bikes. We did not ride the merry-go-round. It looked like the same one which I paid for as a kid, with a thousand attempts to grab the gold ring. I was about thirteen then, and rode a wide handlebar Schwinn around the paths of the park. I was very proud of that balloon-tired beauty. On adventuresome days a friend and I would ride on longer trips, down to the harbor or out to the beach.

One fine afternoon my chum and I "borrowed" a derelict boat from the docks to venture out into the water. It was hardly more than a leaky rowboat, but it had a covered cabin area forward, making it the kind of craft boys dream about. We paddled out into San Diego Bay. I am not sure of our destination, but it does not matter. We could not manage the boat nor paddle back. We panicked. A coast guard launch rescued us, towing us to a concrete amphibian ramp where PBY's trundled down into the water. We were lectured severely. Then I became more concerned about the wrath of my parents than a watery grave or being flogged at the mast. My friend and I sneaked home and were submissive for days. The coast guard never put us on report and our parents never knew of our aspiration toward crime. Today a kid would end up in Juvenile Hall, at the very least.

CHAPTER 14

THE CLUB

I joined the Lookout Mountain Cycle Club, which was a joyous little group of people. The club seemed to function less and less frequently after I became a member. Had I said something wrong?

Then I joined the Denver Bicycle Touring Club. They had a thousand members. Surely I could find a kindred spirit to accompany me on a big tour. This would comfort members of my family, who showed some concern about my riding alone after a heart attack. I signed up with the D.B.T.C. near the end of 1987, after a couple of short rides with their members. We went on some winter "Frostbite Rides" which were designed to keep a rider free of cabin fever through the one-hundred-day months of January and February. The Frostbite Rides were only attempted if roads and paths were free of ice and snow, but they could be very chilly. Sometimes we had only half a dozen eskimos out for a jaunt, as opposed to thirty or forty in the warmer months. I chose to take the shorter, easier rides with this club. It was a new experience riding with a large group of people. I was careful not to crash into someone and humiliate myself.

The club honchos tried to help me find a comrade for long tours. They put an ad in their newsletter. They put a recorded message about my intended travels on their hotline. They even let me give a five-minute talk at a meeting. My plea fell on deaf ears. They just sat there and looked at me with blank stares. I could find no takers.

My requirements for a companion were not all that tough. I was looking for someone like Arnold Schwarzenegger, William F. Buckley, or Racquel Welch. The desirable attributes of these candidates are manifest. Arnold could protect you from villainous types lurking behind shrubs, Bill could spark conversations in the campsite, and Racquel could cook. When I mentioned something about cooking to Bill Humphrey, the hotline announcer, he said, "I think we had better downplay that. It sounds like you want a scullery maid."

"That's up to you, but I'm not totally helpless. I'm good with olives."

I belatedly learned of a three-day, Fourth of July tour in Wyoming which the D.B.T.C. was to sponsor. The route was called the "Cowboy Loop." It was to start in Laramie, go west up over Snowy Range Pass to Saratoga, south to Walden, Colorado, and back to Laramie. There would be a sag wagon, for support and luggage transport. I had missed the registration deadline, so I called the tour leader, Jake Holloway, to see if the planners could tolerate one more rider. He said they still had room and gave me numbers to call for a car ride to Laramie. I called a lady on the list. We'll call her Sweets. "Sweets, my name is Bob and I'm looking for a way to get me and my bike up to Laramie. Jake said to call you."

"Oh yes, well, er, we might have room. Right now there are just two of us going in my car. One more might be O.K. What sort of rider are you?"

"What do you mean?"

"Are you an experienced cyclist?"

"Yes, moderately so. I have done some touring, but I just joined your club last winter."

"Are you a fast rider?"

"No, I'm not super fast. But I'm not pokey, either. What are you looking for?"

"My friend and I are usually in the front third. We hate to get saddled with slow companions. It's a drag waiting for them to appear for the journey back home." Now she had me worried. Was I tying up with a bunch of gunners? I had observed girl bikers who could destroy me if I tried to keep apace. It was like my first fear of the Crazies, all over again.

"I really don't know how to respond to your concerns. I have only been on little rides with the club. I don't know how fast the people will go in Wyoming. I haven't met or ridden with any of them."

"My friend and I like to move right along."

"Do you know Lois Burkart or Dave Grimes?" I asked.

"Yes."

"I have ridden a bit with them. Why don't you call either of them for an objective opinion about how I ride? I will call you again Wednesday evening to see what you think." That ought to impress Sweets. Lois and Dave are tough riders.

"O.K."

Sweets called me Tuesday evening. "I forgot all about another friend who wants to go and this is awkward, but I . . .."

"Hey, no problem. I'm sure to find a ride with someone."

I rode to Laramie in the sag wagon, with Linda and Floyd O'Kelley. Their vehicle arrived in front of my house, resplendent. It was a Sunbeam Funwagon nicknamed "Finnigan." I listened patiently to Linda during the ride north as she enumerated Finnigan's virtues. It had a Commer chassis, a Toyota engine and transmission. I watched Floyd grapple with the Porsche shifter, which worked "opposite hand" and I wondered who might be rescuing whom.

We checked in at the motel and went to our assigned quarters. One of my roommates was already there. He and I retired and were quickly asleep. Late at night, there was a loud knock and the third occupant appeared, beer in hand. We stumbled around rearranging beds and mattresses and bikes and luggage. I slept on the floor. When I left the room the next morning, I caught a glimpse of three bikers already on their way. I went down to have breakfast. There were two gigantic new tour buses waiting to transport easterners west. I talked to two little old ladies traveling in them from New York as I finished my meal. It was 7:30 A.M. and Jake had scheduled a meeting for 9:00. I got my bike and went to find him. He was outside talking to more of the bus tourers.

"This is very difficult for me, to wait like this," I said. "Would you mind if I got on the road now?"

"Type A, huh?" He laughed.

"Classic, but that's only part of it."

"Sure. It's all right. Go ahead."

I rode west on Highway 130 toward the mountains. It was a fine day, but a head wind was already building. At Centennial I found the three riders having breakfast. I introduced myself and ordered apple pie a la mode. I left before they did and spooked some antelope as I climbed out of town. This was a classy ride with all of the astounding views in Wyoming—big open plains, rolling hills and rock formations, gently stepped tundra at higher elevations, and magnificent rock and snow up close in the real range. The newly paved road climbed to

10,800 feet. The gradient decreased near the top, which is unusual for a big pass. It was so good not to have a huge load, just the handlebar bag. I stopped on a bridge and waited for a cyclist to overhaul me. It was Kurt Koerth. I offered him some grapes. We talked and he took off before I did, out of the saddle. I looked at the minuscule cluster on his freewheel and shuddered. Gearheads call it a "corncob."

Kurt and I played leapfrog for several miles, stopping to admire views which we liked. I saw his bike parked by a tavern far down on the west side so I pulled in also. We each drank two beers and I chanced a microwaved burrito. I had discovered a kindred spirit of sorts, another beer drinker. Kurt was the first to pull away from our rest stop. I started to follow and a young kid blasted by. I said hello but got no response, which was annoying. He must have annoyed Kurt also, because I saw him jump hard in pursuit. There was no way I could catch either one. The kid was not from our group.

I arrived at our destination about fourth or fifth, both that day and the next. It isn't supposed to be a race, but I had been pushing it a little because Sweets had intimidated me. We had a group of nice normal friendly people with all degrees of riding experience. Two or three were exceptional riders. Kurt was probably the strongest. I never saw Sweets during the day, only at dinner.

On day two, some of us took a one-mile side trip over to Encampment. We visited a little museum there, looked at an old aerial tramway used to transport ore, and admired a two-story, two-holer outhouse. It was an in-line model, which gave some viewers concern. Our guide explained that the upper level was for use only when snow was over ten feet deep, which reassured the worriers.

The third day, when I returned from breakfast in Walden, one of my roomies announced that he was going to skip the meal and get on his way. I fiddled around for awhile, packing my things and carrying stuff to the sag wagon. I felt a little sad because I had not ridden along at all with either of my fellow room occupants, so I decided to give chase. I passed three or four bikers before reaching Cowdrey, but they were not the right one. At Mountain Home, I said, "This guy is an animal." I could not catch him. The road back was nothing like the pass on the first day, but you did have to climb. It was no piece of cake. I went in a restaurant and found some of our group, but he was not there. No one had seen him.

I decided to forget the pursuit and just coast the downhill. At Woods Landing the highway turns out into the flat with a long gentle slope into Laramie. I caught a tail wind. It was perfect, right square on my back, and it was strong. None of our group was at the motel in Laramie. I waited an hour for the first cyclists to pull in. Referring to the wind, one said, "I thought I had died and gone to heaven." It took two hours for everyone to assemble. My roommate had decided to take time for breakfast after all and I had passed him in Walden, in the first block. Finnigan performed like a champ.

In early June of 1989, the D.B.T.C. advertised a Half-century Sanctioned Patch Ride to Brighton, Colorado, and back. This was not a warning that the cyclist's effort would last for fifty years, but only for fifty miles. I am not much into patches, but by riding measured distances you can earn colorful emblems to attach to your sportswear. Available are patches representing Quarter, Half, Metric, Three-Quarter, and Century bicycle rides. The patches can be sewn together to represent a specific motif and some bikers have jackets covered with memorabilia. At two dollars a crack for each little design, Jacob's coat-of-many-colors can become an expensive as well as ambitious costume.

I elected to try this ride through north Denver and the Platte River Valley, but I showed up late and had to assemble my bike in a hurry to join about forty others waiting in a parking lot at the Houston Fine Arts Center. I had trouble inserting the front wheel hubs past my front rack assembly and felt like a klutz struggling to get everything in place and adjusted. Most of the group started on the journey while I was signing in. I finally got on the bike and raced to catch up, passing small clusters of riders. The leaders were racing with pizazz and authority, I thought, pointing out road hazards and signaling for turns. They appeared to know what they were doing. Every time we started up from a pause at an intersection, however, I was startled by loud reports. It was almost like pistol fire. Were we being shot at by irate citizens of northeast Denver? Then I determined the source of the noise. It was my fellow riders' specially mated shoes and pedals connecting to each other with a sharp crack.

After a few miles, our leaders pulled up short at an intersection, paused, and announced they were lost. We all had maps, but I had not been looking at mine, trusting the skill of those ahead. Then the group sort of disintegrated, riders starting out on their own to explore. There were diverse opinions on how best to find Brighton. I eventually discovered the proper route and it was a very pleasant ride. We met in a restaurant for lunch, each one in his own good time. The ride back was on a different route and people paid more attention to their maps.

It occurred to me, after this little jaunt, that I should assemble some statistics on rides which I had made, if not a collection of patches. My journal records distance data for overnight tours but it has no information for one-day rides or my trips on the Destroyer. For the ten-year period after 1979, the distances traversed on long tours go like this:

Ride Mileage for One Day	Number of Days
40 to 49	6
50 to 59	6
60 to 69	17
70 to 79	15
80 to 89	22
90 to 99	24
100 to 109	26
110 to 119	25
120 to 129	11
130 to 139	2
140 to 149	1
150 or more	1

That's the equivalent of over five months on the road. It covers 14,315 miles. Most of the riding was done with a full complement of touring gear. Perhaps there should be some sort of award for accomplishing one hundred centuries on a bicycle, say a diamond-studded patch or maybe a Ferrari. That would stir my interest. Investment grade diamonds only, please. The color of the car could be your choice.

CHAPTER 15

THE BIG RIDE

All we ask is that you give it a try for three months," Bud said.

"But I don't know anything about managing property," I said.

"It's just solving problems. You can solve problems. I suppose that I could write out a job description, but you will do fine without it."

I managed our two little office buildings for a year. I collected rent and paid bills and tried to keep the tenants happy. They would ask me to paint a room, I would say we were not obligated according to the lease, and I would then paint the room anyway. Mostly I was a coolie. I replaced sprinkler heads, repaired quarry tile, refinished woodwork, patched the roof, shoveled snow, and pruned trees. I hung, taped, and finished drywall. I cleaned ceilings, pulled weeds, and moved electrical fixtures. I "poor boyed" every task, just like Bud and Arch would, to keep the costs on our investment low. The worst chore was lying on my back pruning a twenty-year growth of pfitzers from around the buildings so people could see out their windows. It was hot, prickly, dirty work which I could tolerate for only a few hours each day in the cool of the morning. I did that for two months, hacking away with loppers. On Mondays, I mowed the lawn at home. On weekends, I went to Estes and ran a chain saw.

All of this physical activity was a great novelty for a former desk jockey, for awhile. I developed tendonitis in both elbows. The only way to get relief was to visit the doctor for a shot in the arm. He would only do one at a time. I went to Arch and said, "I've been at this for a year. I have to get away. I want to do the bike trip east. Will you cover for me?"

"How long will it take?"

"One month, plus or minus a few days."

"Sure. I'll take over. Have you ever considered taking up golf?"

I wrote letters to fraternity brothers, friends, and relatives warning them of my intended tour east. When they replied, I planned a tentative route which would put me into nineteen new states. I bought some goodies: touring shoes, tires, tubes, a front rack, two more panniers, and a computer, which is really just a glorified speedometer/odometer. I dismembered an atlas, retaining about half of the maps in a plastic bag. On May 4, 1988, with a wonderful mixture of cortisone and xylocaine in my elbows, I headed east out of Denver on my two-wheeler.

Joes, Colorado, May 5. Joes is a little sneeze of a place in the plains. I am through it in one breath. I do a one-eighty and ride back to the cafe. It does not seem the same as it was when Bob Forrest and I entered years ago to buy cigarettes. (We had been pheasant hunting then and both of us had quit smoking that morning. Our resolve lasted until about eleven o'clock.)

I look at the lunch menu. The proprietor takes my order to the cook and returns to sit at the counter and read his newspaper. "Is this place new?" I ask. "I remember walking up some steps." He turns to look at me as if I have brain damage.

"There they are." He nods and I look out a window to the west. A mass of old cracked concrete pokes through the weeds, stairs leading to nowhere. I try to establish some credibility.

"The *Denver Post* had a recent article about your town winning the state basketball championship back in '29. Did you see it?"

"Yeah, we saw it."

"That must have been a delight, to whip all the big schools in the state." In those days, there were no classifications or divisions according to school size.

"It was no big thing. Our boys had an advantage."

"What was that?"

"We didn't have a basketball floor, just dirt."

I ponder that for a moment.

"I think I understand. They couldn't put the ball on the ground?"

"You got it. If they dribbled, the ball went every whichways. They had to pass."

"A passing team is a winning team."

I chuckle to myself as I ride out of town. I bet every teen-age boy in Joes was on that basketball team.

U.S. 36, Western Kansas, May 6. East of Bird City, Terry Ferstle and I pull to a stop behind a big van with a yellow sign saying "Caution, Runner Ahead." Terry and I teamed up to fight the winds together for a couple of days. He has toured from Oregon. We chat for a few minutes with Doug Walker, who is running across America for the Head Injury Foundation. We pass the van and I have a flat before we go a mile. A goathead is in my tire. Terry comes over by some railroad tracks to help me change the tube. He leans his bike against a post, like I did. Doug Walker runs past us down the highway. I pull and shove and Terry steadies my bike. It's easier with two sets of hands. I wipe off grease and we prepare to leave. Terry has a flat. He has set his rear tire down in thorns. Kansas can be prickly. We reverse roles and get his tire inflated. When we pass Doug again, I shout, "At this rate you'll get there before we do."

Red Cloud, Nebraska, May 7. It is the end of a 121-mile day. Terry and I parted east of Norton after dodging a huge rattler wriggling across the highway. I need a shower badly, but all the motels are full for a Willa Cather Day reunion. After quizzing the locals, I find a hotel and struggle up a long steep flight of stairs carrying the bike. The hall shower does not work so I resort to a makeshift bath at the sink in my room.

Winterset, Iowa, May 10. I take a picture of the hip-roofed little white house which was the birthplace of John Wayne, but the two-dollar entry fee turns me off. Anne will be critical, but my priorities are different. I see two uniformed men leave a cafe north of the town square, so I ride over and carefully lean my bike against the glass. The place is packed, so I turn to leave. The manager says, "There is a place to sit at the back."

"I'm concerned about my bike. I guard it with my life."

"I'll watch your bike. We don't allow any hanky-panky here."

I walk to the back, conscious of many stares at my red shorts. I order a grilled cheese sandwich and a bowl of homemade beef and vegetable soup. The soup is delicious and chunky, more like a stew. I look to the table adjacent. "What kind of pie is that?"

"Banana. You better try some." I devour a huge piece of pie and ask for the check. The whole deal is $2.50. I like the food. I like the price even better.

Des Moines, Iowa, May 10 and 11. I haul into the city, racing two kids down Fleur Drive. I have a little trouble at first, but burn them on the downgrade. Don Dunn is taking care of me. He is head of the Iowa Hospital Association and is the most thoughtful man I know. We drive to Sioux City the next day so he can give a speech. I have lunch with Bob Hoefer and run into Jim Hassenger, my lifeguard partner in high school. Don and I drive back, admiring the countryside. Iowa is *not* flat. "I have to go to Iowa City tomorrow," Don says. "If you can get there on your bike, I'll sneak you into my motel room."

"How far is it?"

"A little over a hundred miles."

"I'll try, but I don't want to get you in trouble. I can pay for the room."

"We have to beat the system."

Interstate 80, Eastern Iowa, May 12. I have made it here from Des Moines by riding 163, 225, and 85. I have jinked around new construction and now I am frustrated by another detour. I enter a service station near Exit 225.

"Isn't there a service road heading toward Iowa City?" I ask.

"Nothing that's paved and you can't ride the interstate."

"There are no signs on the ramps prohibiting bikes. Where *can* I go?"

"You'll have to go up to 6."

"That's ridiculous."

"Well, you can't . . ."

"Watch me."

I get on I-80 and go like hell. Clouds of dust surround me. Dump trucks are pounding down a dirt road on the right. I can hardly see. I wonder if drivers can see me. In fifteen minutes I am off the interstate at Exit 230, heading south.

Earlville, Illinois, May 14. I am sitting on a wood porch at a lovely campground owned by Marilyn and John Urso. She has handed me a huge toddy. "It's grapefruit juice and rum. It makes you feel healthy," she said. My tent is set up on the grass below and I have showered. She won't let me pay for the campsite and has invited me up for the cocktail hour. The Urso's have a "thing" about bicyclists. I have discovered that there are no motels on Highway 92 or U.S. 34 in Illinois. They are all up on the interstate. I laughed all morning on 92 which I dubbed "Near Deer Alley." All the farms have two fake deer in their front lawn. The farmers grow and mow their grass right down in the ditches. Now I am admiring a glittering horse sculpted from automobile bumpers. It can't get away because it is chained to the porch.

Potato Creek State Park, Indiana, May 16. I am freezing my buns in the tent. The temperature has dropped at least twenty degrees since I argued with a ranger at the gate. I tried to start a crusade, but was charged $8.50 anyway. Why so expensive? All I do is bend a few grass blades. I got past Gary all right, but the trucks on U.S. 6 were not giving me room even when they had it to spare. Aren't they accustomed to bikes here? I have got to call home and tell them where I am. How many days has it been? The long-distance lines in Illinois were all shut down.

Menefee's Camp Sack-In, U.S. 20, Near Indiana-Ohio State Line, May 17. I made it into Michigan today, north on 13 and back down on 9. The seven miles west of I-69 on U.S. 20 is the worst piece of junk I have ever seen. I am being terrorized by trucks. I am told that they are not using the interstates, which are junk too. The trucks are down on the secondaries where I am, 6 and 20, in order to avoid tolls and highway repairs. East of Angola I pass a horse-drawn cart full of Amish girls. I stick out my right arm and give them a "thumbs up." They all wave. What a trust in God to clop, clop, clop down this dangerous highway!

Exit 11 Budget Motel, Interstate 80, Ohio, May 19. I am drenched. My panniers have pools in them. The sleeping bag is wet. My clothing in plastic bags is still dry. Advised not to take 303. I did anyway. It is lovely at first, on the west end; tough east of Brunswick— steep hills and *heavy* rain.

North Springfield Campground, Pennsylvania, May 20. I feel like a turkey. I negotiate with Doug Bannister to get him down to seven dollars from nine. Then his mom, Virginia, sends up rhubarb pie and other good things to eat. I can't see Lake Erie well from my tent site or identify a horizon. It's too foggy.

Cazenovia, New York, May 23. Awful steep hills on U.S. 20. I sweat buckets.

Points of Interest/Mileage: Sore tits, 107.

Kirkside Motor Lodge, Bennington, Vermont, May 25. Soaked. Hypothermic. Best motel in world. Wash out gear under downspout. Kind owner gives me plastic bags to protect room. Everything spread out to dry.

Concord, New Hampshire, May 26. Heavily dressed for cold. Didn't know about hill. Ride in icy sweat through fog to Wilmington for breakfast.

The above is just an overview, but you can probably sense how my desire was ebbing. The only thing that made this trip tolerable was the frequent respites with friends along the way. They gave me a goal. In fact, I had a series of goals. I did not know anything about the East and was a bit intimidated by this trip. Friends, and strangers, took me in and kept me pumped up. I surprised one couple only. Barbara and Jerry Korn invited me to Limerick, Maine, after I called. I had not seen Barbara since high school. We had a beautiful, nostalgic evening. Barbara surprised me with the fact that I had been in her kindergarten class. Now, *that's* a memory.

Barbara and Jerry were concerned about me the next day. They were afraid I could not make it all the way to Bristol and that I would be confused by the complexity of the roads. They helped me load my equipment in their car and drove me to Gray. This gave me about a twenty- or thirty-mile head start.

I stopped in Brunswick for an ice cream cone. A young man approached me.

"Have you come fah?" he asked.

"Pardon me?"

"Have you come fah?"

"I came from Denver."

"That's *fah!*" My mind flipped back to the little kids whom I failed to impress in a South Dakota motel room and I was not listening well when he advised me to cut over to Bowdoin College.

I arrived in Bristol at 2:00 P.M. after a short sixty-three-mile day. It was Saturday, May 28th, the first day of Memorial Day weekend. I had covered 2,339 miles in twenty-four riding days plus one day off. The first leg of my journey was complete.

I had a preplanned route for the first part. There were a few deviations, due to wind, detours, and traffic. I had not selected roads for the leg to Washington. I would go by dead reckoning, and hope that the title was not a harbinger of things to come. I had a pleasant one-day suspension with my cousin Helen Lent and her husband, Ray I had last seen Helen when I was ten years old. With this pattern, I will see her again when I am 110. They were reluctant to let me start on the tail of the holiday weekend, but I insisted that I leave on Monday.

I started at about 7:30. I went back south on U.S. 1, which all the easterners call Route 1. Traffic was light in the morning and I had no problem on the open stretches. When I rode into a congested area, it was a different story. Two drivers pulled out in front of me and another opened her door in my path to exit from her car. None of them had seen me. Down near Kennebunkport, the traffic increased. Everyone must have come over to visit George Bush. I passed strings of cars, one or two hundred at a time, on their right side. I was very watchful for a passenger swinging a door at me, but it was a delight to buzz on through while they sat there pissed. I wheeled into North Hampton, New Hampshire, at about 5:15 after 121 miles and one flat tire.

I skirted wide to the west of Boston, over through Concord on 62. Once I almost ran into a huge tree growing right on the edge of this old road in suburbia. I wandered south, caught a corner of Rhode Island and went west to Hartford through heavy rain on U.S. 44 and Alternate 44. I had another flat in Hartford. I was not paying attention west of there, so I went on a little side trip up the hills to Burlington. I had still another flat. I took 69 south to U.S. 6, then pedaled west.

I could not find an empty motel in Brewster, New York. A lady there said, "I can let you have a little room in back, but it's pretty trashed out."

"How much will it be?"

"Forty dollars."

"You mean that you would charge me forty dollars for a trashed out room?"

"Yes."

"No you won't."

I was disgusted, but I had some time left, so I headed south on U.S. 202. Then I was in serious difficulty. The road and traffic got worse. It was rush hour. The drivers were hostile. The light was fading and so was I. It was scary. I had to get off the road. The map of this area was at a very small scale and I had no idea how far it was to some civilization where I could find lodging. I went by a long stone wall. It had a few openings secured by a single chain. I passed a two-story building which appeared to be abandoned. I stopped, turned, and rode back. I ducked under the chain and pushed my bike to a grassy yard between the building and the stone wall. I quickly stripped the bike, laid it under a hedge, and set up my tent. I had to mash the grass, which was about two feet deep. I shoved my bags in the tent and crawled in. I was secure.

I removed my shoes, arranged the panniers against the tent walls, and got comfortable. I could see through the screened flaps what appeared to be a running track. This was a school yard of some sort. I poured an inch of vodka into an aluminum cup and carefully cut two slices of cheddar. I groped for my patch kit and started to work on punctures.

Lights came on in the building. I listened intently and heard the murmur of voices. I reasoned that it was almost dark and my tent would probably not be seen from a window. I blew on the patching cement to dry it. Then I heard shouts and running feet. A troop of young blacks was staring at my tent opening.

"What you dooin', man? You can't camp here."

"Yeah," another said. "This is private property." Silence. I did not know what to say, so I said nothing.

"Aw, come on. It's jus' an old man and a bike." They disappeared as quickly as they had come. I gulped the rest of the vodka and reflected. Where could I go now? It's too late to pack up and move. And to where? I never ride in the dark and don't want to learn how now. I decided to continue patching in the beam of my flashlight. Then I heard a new voice.

"Hey, out there. It's cool. You can stay. Nobody will bother you."

"Thank you," I answered.

I crossed the Hudson River for the second time, rode through Bear Mountain State Park and into New Jersey on Highway 94. I crossed the Delaware River on a footbridge in the third Portland of my journeys. Then I headed south on 611 and turned west on 113 to avoid Philadelphia. This road started well with easy pedaling through a pretty valley. It got worse. The paving went sour and any shoulder present was full of rubble. I was thinking that I was fortunate to be on this mess during a low density Saturday when a dump truck came up behind me and hung on. He held position stubbornly and gave me a long dirty horn blast. There was no oncoming traffic. When he finally passed I shouted my favorite obscenity up at his open window. The truck pulled over and stopped ahead of me partly on the highway and partly on the shoulder. A second truck came up from behind and did the same. I slowed to a stop. I was boxed. The driver jumped down from the front vehicle and walked toward me.

I figured that I was about to be hammered. I decided to stay astride my bike. The only good omen was that the driver of the second truck stayed in his cab.

"What did you say to me?" the truck driver asked.

"You heard what I said. If you want to blow me off the road, you better do it with your rig. Your horn isn't gonna cut it."

"You're a terrible hazard and shouldn't be out on the road."

"I'm not as big a hazard as the way your trucks are parked. If you want me off the road, then get your nifty highway department to build a shoulder I can ride."

"I don't want you on the shoulder. I want you outa here—gone. You have no right to be on the highway at all. You don't pay the taxes." And on, and on, and on. With every word it became more obvious that this guy was not going to take a shot at me. I think he was taken aback when he got a good look at my face and discovered my age. I had grown a beard by then and it was white. We exchanged a few more barbs and he walked back to his truck.

I entered Washington, D.C., on U.S. 1. When I saw the imposing white dome to my left I turned onto North Capitol Street. I took some photos and then rode slowly down Constitution Avenue to the Vietnam Memorial. I was not allowed to take my bike down the ramp so I leaned it against a bench and walked down with my camera. I quickly snapped two shots. Then I saw a man tracing the name of a buddy. A tightness developed far back in the roof of my mouth and all of a sudden I could not see very well. I could not take a picture of the tracer.

I ate a hot dog and downed a soft drink and just stood around smiling foolishly at everyone. I wanted to shout, "Hey, I just dropped in from Denver. It sure is good to be here. You have no idea how good. You ought to see your country out there. It's doing fine." No one paid any attention to me.

I crossed the Potomac and took a bike path south, past scores of joggers and a few other bikers. I could not figure out how to get to Highway 244. I crossed streets and dodged traffic and ended up in the Pentagon parking lot. I asked a lady at one gate for directions and queried two officers leaving their cars, but no one knew the location of 244. If only I had asked about the Columbia Pike. I did not know how to communicate.

I decided to chance a freeway curving west. I got on and cranked hard, trying to shorten the time of exposure. A highway patrolman passed. I saw him stop ahead, just past a ramp marked "244 East." He was watching me. I turned toward the off ramp. Another sign said, "244 West, One-half Mile." Wary of the cop, I started down the ramp, but then saw his car ease out and pull away. I made a hard left, to cut back up onto the freeway and go for the proper exit. Instead, my front tire peeled off and I bounced right down on the paving in a heap. This was my first spill in many years of adult bicycling. I had crashed once into the back of a parked truck, but that doesn't count. That was embarrassing, but it was not a spill. When I finally dumped in Virginia, due to a dumb old flat, I was sorrowfully injured with ouchie-bites. I had road rash about the size of a dime on one knee and a nick in one finger. Poor baby.

I called Sy Wilhelmi for direction to his house in Annandale. He and Charlotte were very good to me while I waited to board a plane home. Sy dropped me off at the mall one day so I could walk to all the historic monuments and visit museums. I hurried through five museums, got lost in one, and had a wonderful day. At the Air and Space Museum I admired Grumman's lunar module and an F4F. I took a picture of a picture of a *Yellow Peril,* to show my kids. I looked at a photo of young George Bush, smiling from the cockpit of his TBM. Then I saw an incredible sight.

Before me, encased in glass, was a model of the nuclear-powered CVN-65, the USS *Enterprise.* Detail work on the eleven-foot replica was exquisite, including a full complement of aircraft parked on the flight and hangar decks. The model took twelve years to complete with a commitment of about a thousand hours each year. The dedicated builder was Stephen Henninger. I walked slowly around the display, admiring the dozens of meticulously crafted planes with their folded wings. Without the planes this model would have been superb, with them it was awesome. I thought about the years devoted to this cause and compared them to my own campaign. Mr. Henninger and I might have something in common. If I could hang in for one more long tour in the coming year, and could somehow scoop up the rest of the states, I would complete my goal in twelve years also. But I was surely not putting in Steve's kind of hours. Quite by accident I would later discover that he lived about thirty miles north of me in Boulder and we would talk. He had started the model in Peru, then shipped it to the U.S., where he had to build a wing on his house trailer to enclose the ship. Others have built boats in their basement or back yard, but an aircraft carrier is special.

I finally tore myself away from the *Enterprise* and walked upstairs where I could stand on a mock-up bridge listening to the sounds of jets landing and watching them hit the arresting cables. Then, as I passed a full-size F6F, I heard bright sounds. I hurried outside. The U.S. Army "Blues" were playing Glenn Miller's version of "American Patrol." It was a fitting end to a long excursion across our country.

I shipped my bike without boxing in the same plane which I rode home. I wrote USAir to tell them how pleased I was that they took good care of my friend and me. I also wrote the following letter:

An open letter of "Thanks" to: Don Dunn, Des Moines, IA; Barbara Dunn, Des Moines, IA; Bob Hoefer, Sioux City, IA; Jane and Dave Maehr, Davenport, IA; Marilyn and Don Wood, Clarendon Hills, IL; M.E. and Jim Collinge, Rochester, NY; Barbara (Henderson) and Jerry Korn, Limerick, ME; Helen and Ray Lent, Bristol, ME; Mary Beth and Ray Dunn, South Lancaster, MA ; Charlotte and Sy Wilhelmi, Annandale, VA

Dear Friends:

On June 6, I arrived in Annandale, VA. via Bristol, ME. My Chinese Thunderbird carried me faithfully for 3,104 miles. The longest day's ride was 137 miles. The shortest, the last, was 44 miles. On 17 of the 32 riding days (I had 2 rest days), I covered over 100 miles. My top speed was 45.5 mph. There were many long cranks at 4 to 8 mph. I lost 10 pounds of body weight somewhere in the 21 states traveled. The 70 pounds of bike plus panniers did not change much. I had 5 flats, 4 of which occurred in the front tire after rotation in Bristol. They, too, got pretty thin.

Without your support, this odyssey could have been a real drag—a fact I suspected before departure. I stayed a night or two in many of your homes. The amenities were much appreciated, but the real lift came from your caring. Since some of you know each other, I have chosen to list everyone above. I will close with a more personalized handwritten description of what happened right after I left you. There are some general comments about this trip which I wish to share with all.

You all know that I was trying to get into as many states as possible as quickly as possible. It is very hard for a single biker to sustain motivation day after day on a long tour. I rode with a young biker, Terry Ferstle, for two days in Kansas under some extremely difficult and hazardous crosswind conditions. We literally pulled each other over the terrain. After we went our separate ways, I was free to do whatever I liked, but the companionship of a compatible rider is usually more desirable than total autonomy. Nevertheless, I later thanked the good Lord many times that, contrary to the original plan, I was a lone rider. I would not have liked the responsibility for the safety of other people or "pumping them up" to push on. I had my own problems.

That's where the help of all you good people came in. An evening with you took my mind off the terrible task ahead and I quit feeling like an ant marching across America.

In spite of my total ignorance about eastern highways, I did manage, by pure chance, to discover some classic bike rides with great paving and magnificent scenery. The best were these: Route 136 from Red Cloud, NE (Willa Cather's home), to Tecumseh, NE; Highway "B" east of Clearmont, MO; the west end of Route 303 in OH; Keene, VT, to

Concord on 9 and 202; Bear Mountain State Park in NY; 94 south through northern NJ; Route 100, PA to DE.

There were some great emotional highs: Seeing Amish families in horse-drawn carts on U.S. 20 in Indiana—talk about living in faith; witnessing the awesome power of Niagara Falls; suffering with others the pain of the Vietnam Memorial; hearing the enthusiastic encouragement of many, many other travelers.

There were depressing lows: Four hours to crank 22 miles into head wind from Bedford to Corning, Iowa; pounding rain south of Cleveland, north of Troy, east of Hartford; gut-wrenching steep hills south of Cleveland (three of which I could not crank) and near the Finger Lakes in New York (which I could crank, but with great sweating effort); rocks, fireworks, and verbal abuse hurled at me by irate motorists who were delayed by two or three seconds.

This tour was not as demanding physically as many other loaded trips I have made in Colorado or out-of-state, due to the lack of heat or mountains. The tour was, however, the riskiest venture I have made on a bike. Traffic was fierce. Some roads were terrible. Truckers were, I discovered, boycotting expressways because of road repairs and high tolls. They were driving on the secondaries, where I was. None of you, thankfully, verbalized the concerns you may have had for my safety. My partner, S.J. Archuleta, who is a strong biker, referred to this ride as a death march. Perhaps his candid appraisal kept me on guard.

I had many frightening close passes by cars and trucks, several abrupt turns in front of me, one avoided head-on collision, and a non-destructive spill (my first in twelve years) on the last day while playing cat-and-mouse with a highway patrolman. During the latter, I was, as on two other occasions, illegally riding a freeway. It was either that or spend the rest of my life touring the Pentagon parking lot. Peace officers were always guardedly courteous to me. I sensed that they resented my presence because it could ruin their whole day.

In spite of the skill and experience of a biker, it is obvious that a brief mental lapse by any one of thousands could cause his demise. It is only the prayers of self and others to a benevolent God which bring any real protection. I am thankful to you for your tolerance and prayers. You have helped me to partially fulfil a dream.

Very truly yours,
Bob Voiland

One incident on this trip deserves further comment. It's the gap up in Maine, between Limerick and Gray. It bothered me for a time, as have small gaps on other tours, because I did not bike the entire distance without help. After all, I had made a promise to myself. The prospect of a gap can be troublesome if you are goal-oriented, Type A, or a Virgo. I am all three.

Arch has told me that I sometimes confuse effort for results. This is a valid statement. Maybe someday I will learn to accept the inevitable in a practical manner. On my tour to the Pacific Northwest, a pickup truck carried me over twenty miles of loose gravel west of Tiger, Washington. Before attempting La Manga and Cumbres passes, I rode with the Crazies in a rain-pelted van for fifteen miles after I had cycled alone by a circuitous route to Antonito. Woody knew that this would disturb me. He asked for my permission to motor down the road. Going to California, the kindness of Mary Lou transported me through a hairy portion of the Glenwood Canyon construction. You will read about another example of direct aid shortly.

There. Now that I have confessed, I feel much better.

CHAPTER 16

YOUR STUFF

I overheard a whisper near me, "Great tan."

"Yes, but look at his feet. They're white. How weird. Why would he wear shoes?"

Bruce and Leslie and I were sitting in a crowd of people on the edge of Whitefish Lake watching a regatta. I wore a swimsuit and T-shirt. Someone had noticed my bizarre coloration. Apparently they were unable to see my hands. If they thought my feet looked funny, a glance at my hands would put them in stitches. I had the telltale biker's circles branded on the back, with a mottling of spots all over my fingers. I never could understand how the gloves stay glued in one precise position well enough to produce the unique design.

Sun on the hands never hurt. Not so for the other parts. I always have a tough time staying greased up. The balms and blocks annoy me. I don't like to take the time to mess with them, but I usually regret it later and end up a hurting zebra.

Bikers are funny looking creatures even without the sunburn. They have a Coca-cola bottle silhouette, emaciated upper body supported by froggy quadriceps. I can lose fourteen pounds on a big tour but still retain a Michelin in my middle. Add pipe cleaner arms to the paint-by-numbers color effects and you can imagine some marvelous reactions at a nude beach.

I am more concerned about rain than the sun. Riding in the rain is a big pain in the wazoo, mostly because of road dirt. I hate to get the bike all muddy. The wetness is no problem to the human frame as long as you can maintain body heat. My body is wet all the time anyway, from perspiration. There are all kinds of rain suits and partially porous fabrics now, but they never seem to breathe or non-breathe in sync with my changing requirements. I would rather get wet, unless its a cold wet.

A lovely girl in a restaurant in Sturgis, Michigan, asked me, "What do you do about rain?"

"I get wet," I said. Later, I was so repentant about my terse, smartass reply to this fellow biker that I delivered a discourse to her longer than the chapter you are reading. She surely did not need that much advice.

Now, you could get hypothermic and that is bad. It has happened to me half a dozen times, but not always in the rain. It can occur quickly on a fast downhill ride off a pass which has burned all of your calories. My poncho is no good for riding but it has come in handy as an instant body wrap to preserve heat. West of Cochetopa Pass I shivered in the poncho as the rain pelted me. I choked down part of a mince meat bar to restore energy and heat. It was not pleasant because I had little water to sluice it down, but I was able to force feed a thousand calories into my system very rapidly. Then I rode on in the rain. Camping in that torrent would have been miserable.

If the water from the sky is hard, as in "hard as hail," get under cover.

If it is snowing, you are working on the wrong sport.

I have been very lucky. Usually the weather has treated me very well. When I return from a trip and report to Anne on my environment she is often surprised. She has tracked my progress and followed the weather reports on radio and TV.

"Boy, you sure are lucky," she would say. Like the man says, I'd rather be lucky than smart.

It does take some smarts, however, to plan a tour. This is probably the place to itemize the goods which I take along. The list is a far cry from the equipment hauled on the Destroyer. I now have with me the following, which include the items worn on my body:

FOR TRAVEL:
1 friendly and trusted bicycle
1 pump
3 water bottles
4 spare tubes
2 patch kits
1 spare rear derailleur cable (with one cropped end)

2 twenty-inch bungee cords
3 nine-inch bungee cords
1 set of tools, including:
    1 four-inch adjustable wrench
    3 open-end wrenches
    2 allen wrenches
    1 spoke wrench
    1 chain rivet extractor
    1 tiny screwdriver
    2 tire irons
    1 dirty old toothbrush
    1 assortment of nuts, bolts, etc.
1 tire valve adapter
1 can of oil
1 set of maps

FOR CAMPING:
1 tent
1 down-filled sleeping bag (mummy style)
1 foam sleeping pad
1 Bluet gas stove with base
1 spare butane cartridge
1 aluminum cooking pot with lid and separate lifting handle
1 aluminum cup
1 insulated plastic cup
1 old beat up grungy G.I. mess kit
1 Swiss army knife
1 fork
1 spoon
1 bottle of detergent
1 pot scrubber
1 dish cloth
1 dish towel
4 packs of matches (packed in separate places)

CLOTHING:
1 helmet with attached mirror
1 spare mirror for attachment to sunglasses
1 cap
1 sweatband
1 pair of cycling gloves

4 T-shirts
2 pair of cycling shorts
2 pair of regular shorts (underwear)
1 sweatshirt
1 Goretex windbreaker with hood (blaze orange)
1 poncho (sometimes)
2 pair of long socks
2 pair of short socks
1 jogging suit (formal attire for dining out)
1 swimming suit and athletic supporter (sometimes)
1 pair of cycling shoes
1 down-filled jacket (sometimes)
1 pair rain pants
1 pair booties

FOR HYGIENE:
1 towel
1 bar of soap
1 deodorant
1 toothbrush
1 toothpaste
2 small packs of tissues
1 small roll of toilet paper
1 safety razor
1 nail clipper
1 comb
1 tube of Vaseline
1 tube of Silvadene
1 lip balm
1 sunscreen
1 insect repellant
1 box of aspirin
6 cotton swabs
1 first-aid kit

MISCELLANEOUS:
1 flashlight
1 pair of bifocals
1 pair of sunglasses
1 journal
2 pencils

1 billfold with credit card, driver's license, blood type, whom
   to notify, money
1 packet of traveler's checques
8 plastic bags with Ziplock closures
3 plastic shower caps (rain protection for front bags)
1 nylon cord
1 camera with extra film
1 tiny New Testament and Psalms
1 paperback novel
1 cable lock (sometimes)
1 fishing device with flies and lures (sometimes)

You are probably wondering how one person can haul all of this
crap. It would be easier with more people along because many items can
be shared. Sometimes, when I lay my stuff out on the living room floor,
I am filled with utter despair. But most of the items are small and light.
I am now using four panniers, two of which are medium size and have
a single zippered exterior pocket on a zippered bag. These are hung
from a standard rear rack. On the front of the bike are the other two panniers, small zippered bags mounted on a Blackburn Lowrider. I also have
a small handlebar bag with a see-through map enclosure. Counting a
stuff sack for my sleeping bag, which is mounted with the tent and pad
on the rear rack, that makes six bags in all. It takes some experimenting
to discover the best way to pack every item for superior balance and a
minimum of nerve-wracking rattles. The Lowrider is a dream because it
centers the load right on the front hub where it will not adversely affect
steering. Shifting weight to the front balances tire wear. After suffering
for many years with dehydration, I now carry three large water bottles.
They are not necessarily filled, depending on the terrain.

Bike nuts will note that my list is short on spare parts and tools. If
I were riding to Alaska, I would maybe carry more. Better yet, I would
team up with a mechanic. I can hardly trim my nails.

I have not yet discussed nourishment. I am a ghastly cook so any
meal prepared by me must be simple. I purchase most of the vittles
along the way, but start a trip with the following basics:

gorp
minute rice
cooking oil
salt and pepper
instant coffee

tea bags
packets of oat meal
packets of dried soups
cheese
crackers
vodka

The purists will be upset by the last item, but I am not out there to suffer. A martini, extremely dry, can smooth the bumps under a sleeping bag. Since I forego carrying a still, the liquor supply in my small plastic bottle is replenished by a scientific procedure called decanting. As the journey continues, I purchase:

peanuts
tuna
sardines
Dinty Moore stew
chili
oriental noodles
seedless grapes, bing cherries, nectarines, bananas, apples
French rolls
peanut butter

For gourmet dining, I eat out. I have never built an open fire while on a bicycle tour. I have never camped out after riding in a heavy rain. Something is invariably soaked and it would be very difficult to dry things inside a tent.

At trip end it is not surprising to find a can of spinach or the like in the bottom of a bag. The increase in transported load due to ardent grocery shopping is offset by my own decrease in body weight due to sweating, reduction in fat, and tired old parts simply falling off. The best way to find me on the highway is to look for a trail of parts.

The camping is not a big thing with me. I am out mostly for the ride. I will admit, however, that sometimes it is very pleasant to stretch out on a cool starlit night, warm and secure in the down bag and protecting canopy. Your goods are all arranged for easy access at the edges of the tent. You have memorized the location of each little thing, knowing that it can be touched in the darkness to bring instant solace. "Let's see now. Water, knife, shoes, Preparation H . . ." George Carlin would be proud of you. You have a place for your stuff.

CHAPTER 17

TWENTY DAYS OF TERROR

February 10, 1989

Dear Arch and Woody,

This may be your last chance. I may quit asking and then you'll be sorry.

On or about April 17, I will fire out of Lakewood on my Chinese Thunderbird for points south and east. The proposed route will go through Limon, Kit Carson, and Lamar into the Oklahoma and Texas panhandles. Then it will wander down toward Florida, hopefully in time to catch Bud before he comes back to Boulder. Do you know his plans?

You are welcome to join me with anyone you choose as long as there is an absence of comments about my red pants.

I think you might find a tour like this challenging. With luck, we might even see an armadillo, which is the Texas state bird.

This is projected to be a trip of about one month, extending into North and South Carolina, and ending in Louisville, Kentucky. However, you do not have to "go all the way" if you have a moral hangup of some sort.

Think about it.

Bob

Woody called first. He said there was no way that he could take off for a month. I told him that we would be going very close to Dallas, that we could ride to there in eight days with a little luck, and he could catch a plane home. He wished me well. Then Arch called. He said I was crazy and that Bud would probably return to Boulder before I even left. We wanted to know if I would come up and help with some grunt work on a building he managed.

Still no takers. This could give a guy a complex. Do I smell bad, or what? Maybe Arch was right. Maybe my sanity was in question. Was the tour into forty-eight states now an obsession? I had only thirteen states to go. At least Portia Masterson thought it was a neat idea. She had put a little squib in the "Self Propulsion News" about my goal. She even sacrificed good copy space for a photo of me. It did not make me rich and famous like she promised, but I received a few positive comments.

When I returned from the big ride to Maine and Washington, D.C., there was an offeror waiting to purchase a partnership interest in the two buildings I had been managing. I was the logical candidate of the four partners to give up his share. I was bored with the task of managing, I did not live in Boulder, and I could use the cash. I sold my interest. Bud, Arch, and Woody were no longer my partners. Now I was out of a job again.

Anne and I went out to see Lisa in Clearwater, Washington. I drove us out of our way a bit in order to observe again some of the places I had biked in that state, Oregon, and Utah. Anne thought it would be wise to omit a visit to Dan in Portland. She believed it would make him sad that we would not be spending any significant amount of time with him. I insisted that we try to find him. We did, and it lifted my spirits tremendously to see that his means, though very modest, were improved. He was more articulate than when I saw him in 1980, but still not as lucid as I would have liked. He was cheery. We took him to lunch and he was grateful for a free meal. He did not seem to resent that we were there for only a couple of hours. We gave him some money and a hug.

We drove west to Astoria and when I turned the car up over the high portion of the bridge spanning the Columbia River, Anne said, "Slow down. This gives me sweaty palms." I tried to tell her how spooky it was on a bike.

I got acquainted with Lisa's big happy dog, Boomer. We took walks on the beach and in the woods. Boomer slobbered all over my clothes when I petted him and we had a swell time. After a little side trip to Seattle with Lisa, Anne and I headed back to Denver. We saw two huge truck trailers blown over by the wind, one in Oregon and one in Wyoming.

Anne tried to stir my interest in a monthly meeting of retired men at our church. I put it off. I did not want to accept the fact that I was retired. I made a half-hearted application for work at McDonald's and another restaurant, but chose to forego that indignity. It wasn't that I thought of the job as degrading. I have done tons of menial work and have sometimes welcomed it. I just did not want my friends to think that I was destitute. I am not, but for the few years since I had been away from engineering, Anne had been concerned about our lack of income. She has not expressed her nervousness as much lately.

I was bereft by the lack of a goal, a purpose for life. The bike thing had become a crutch, which I guess I subconsciously felt would pull me through this void. I finally relented and told Anne that I would attend a meeting of the "retarded" at our church. This made her cross and she said, "Don't berate them or yourself."

I was shocked when I went to the meeting. First of all, one of the men used the same word I had. When I asked, "Is this the place?" He said, "Yep, this is where the retarded gather."

There were way more people at the gathering than I had anticipated, about a dozen. I knew most of them. These were men for whom I had great respect. They had been top dogs, important individuals in their fields. We laughed and bantered and talked about every subject in the world except the one I wanted to discuss—how are you dealing with retirement? I told my share of lies and tried to keep it light. I did not want to show my sadness at the significant waste of horsepower sitting across from me, well-tuned machines with engines idling or totally shut down. If they were revved up, the howl of turbos would be as fine as the start of an Indianapolis 500. We drank too much coffee and when the last doughnut was gone everyone left to go home and putter around the house. Later I gathered nerve to ask a few how they liked their retirement and whether they acquired that status by choice. The answers were all affirmative. Either I did not fit in with that group or they were not being candid with me.

If they were telling me the truth, then most retirees must not have to deal with the junk that was running through my head. Maybe those guys were just tougher than I was, or more serene. Like the Destroyer, I needed strokes. Why was recognition so important? It's just vanity, I told myself. It's wrong to be vain. Surely I should be able to muster *some* self-worth, without an ego boost, without the praise of others. If not, I never should have left my company so soon.

Then I questioned my past career and the education preceding it. Why was I so ill equipped to adapt to change? I could plan a pass through the weeds to find pheasants, but I could not plan my life. I was unable to deal with the pain of finding a new direction.

I hate a quitter, but I had dealt with that guilt earlier and realized that the "no quit" ethic can create a trap. Sometimes it is better to look for a new avenue. I had empathy for Tom Landry, who was caught in the trap. He wanted to make the Cowboys go one more time. It was not to be.

The only other thing of import that I ever quit was the Navy. Had that been a mistake? Was my recent preoccupation with F6F's and Cal Swanson some indication of remorse over that score? Would the Navy have prepared me any better for change? "No, we've been over that," I postulated. "I probably would have augured in somewhere."

While I was waiting for winter to be over, I shoveled snow and picked up dog poop. I was disgusted when I caught myself dragging out little chores so I would have something to do the next day. Anne gave me a new shovel for Christmas, a Back-Saver™ model with bent handle. I liked it better than the old steel shovel I kept repairing. I prayed for snow but was careful not to admit it to anyone. When my neighbors saw me throwing snow they expressed their concern and offered me their new snow blowers. I declined and kept shoveling. Would I have to buy one of those expensive machines just so the neighbors would not have to worry about me?

My major medical insurance was not worth a dime. Since my heart attack, the companies considered me an unacceptable risk. It was difficult to find a company which would insure me at all and the one I finally found insisted on a rider deleting coverage for any condition arising from "cardiac and/or vascular disorders." I was assured by the company's representative that they would drop this rider after three years elapsed from the date of my problem. We were going on five years and they had only partially relented, even with substantial praise of my health by my doctor. He wrote a positive letter, more reassuring than I would have drafted, but it did not guarantee that I would remain free of sickness and live forever. The insurance company deleted the words "and/or vascular." They seem to have forgotten that they are in business to insure against risk. They want risk to go away. It ain't gonna happen.

Wouldn't it be a good joke on me if I got so mad at the insurance company that I caused myself to have another heart attack?

I had a few medical expenses during 1988, about six hundred dollars worth, mostly related to a search for relief from "tennis elbow." I have not played tennis for twenty years. I thought I would test my insurance company a little and submit a claim against my five-hundred-dollar deductible policy. The company waffled. They were reluctant to part with eighty dollars or so and sent back questionnaires. With regard to the fishing fly embedded in my finger they wanted to know, "Does this claim involve an injury?" and "Was the claimant injured at work?" I try to be a decent sort of sportsman but when I have a fish on the line I do not have the stones to tie on a second hook and stick it into my body to provide a fair fight. I seldom fish at work.

While I was paddling to and fro in this sea of self-pity, two things happened which made me reflect on my situation even more deeply. The first had to do with the planning for my projected bike trip. I sent out five letters. One was to Bud and, as Arch had predicted, Bud replied that he would not be in Florida when I was scheduled to arrive there. Two letters went to friends of Anne whom I did not know. One lady in Chattanooga, Joy Kendall, replied with a gracious invitation to stay with her family, as did the other, but Joy requested an itinerary of my tour so they could "follow" along. Up to that point, my planning had been very general, only detailed enough to discover folks along the way whom Anne or I knew. I sat down with an atlas and searched for a reasonable route through each of the thirteen states. Then I transferred my marks to a plain unmarked map of the United States. I was aghast at what I saw. All of the states were hooked on my line, like fish on a streamer, but I had just barely "caught" most of them. With the exception of a beeline from Santa Rosa Beach, Florida, to Chattanooga, my proposed route was a very efficient smooth arc. I had chosen the shortest possible path for the given requirements. Once again, I was going to slight a lot of beautiful country.

I questioned whether I subliminally wanted to quickly end this campaign, just get it over. Was it no longer any fun? Had the last trip east made me road shy? I had made a promise to myself and I was going to keep it if it killed me, but something was telling me to keep the miles of exposure as low as possible. Then, I vacillated. All of this negative thinking was nonsense. I could take my time for a change, be careful, and also have fun. I am still lucky. If it turns out that I am no longer lucky, the retirement problem ceases to be a problem.

The other happening had to do with a fantastic book. I did not even pay attention to its title, at first. Lisa had been reading this book when Anne and I visited her. She gave a copy to Anne for Christmas. Anne raced through the book, which was no surprise to me. She is a very fast reader. Anne then said, "This is the best book I have ever read." This was a surprise. Anne is not given to exaggeration. I picked up the book and read the first line. It really grabbed me. Then I ratio-nalized that it was just my aversion to snakes.

I started to read the book. I am a slow reader, usually, but I was motoring right along. I identified with one of the major characters, then said to Anne, "Who do you think I might be in this story?"

"Call," she said.

She got that right. The book was Larry McMurtry's *Lonesome Dove*. Captain Woodrow Call has his problems. He is a stoic workaholic. He fixes on a goal and he will not let go. He does not know how to have fun. He is a loner, uncommunicative, and difficult to be around. These are just his minor faults, of course. It isn't until near the end of the story that you learn what a real jerk he is. He can't level with his son, he does not know how to love anyone except a business associate. Clara berates him and tries to point him in the proper direction. He will not be turned.

Well, Captain, don't feel like the Lone Ranger. I would have drug that rotten old corpse to the Guadalupe, the Picketwire, the Ganges, or anywhere McCrae wanted to go.

I was pretty much a mess waiting for winter to end.

I reached Hugo, Colorado, the first day with a moderate tail wind pushing me south. On day two I fought through a head wind to Lamar. I was on the road for eleven hours to cover 102 miles. The third day I was favored again by a tail wind which blew hard in the morning but trailed off as I approached Boise City, Oklahoma. It was a seven-hour ride over ninety-eight miles. See the difference the wind makes? The phenomenon was as if two giants with vacuum clean-ers were sweeping the plains from south and north on alternate days.

True to the pattern, a heavy gale faced me as I rode into the Texas panhandle. At Dumas, I gave up my planned route through Amarillo and headed east, eager for the respite of even a cross wind. Surely the wind will die tomorrow, I thought. That was a mistake. The south wind kept on. I had also left the generous shoulder of U.S. 287 and was confronted by an increasing number of hills in the cap rock coun-try, sandstone formations studded with oil and gas wells. The giant on the north was having his way with me. When the road jogged south, I was lucky to make six miles an hour, geared down even on the flat. Both the Cimarron and Canadian rivers had depressed me with their minuscule trickles of water.

On the morning of the sixth day, I left Wheeler, Texas, before dawn in an all-out effort to beat build-up of the wind and fight my way

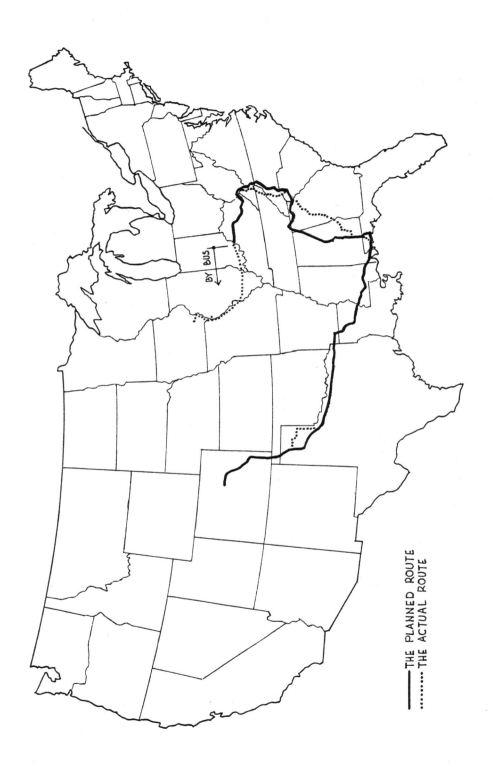

BY BUS

——— THE PLANNED ROUTE
·········· THE ACTUAL ROUTE

south to Highway 287. Bob Frankenberry, a Texaco dealer, spent some time with me the evening before, helping me examine road options. I was in Childress at 1:30, having crossed the Red River which had a respectable flow but nothing like the quantity its banks had once held. Then it got hot. I stopped eight times in the last thirty miles west of Quanah. An RV driver offered me a Pepsi at a rest stop, but I declined. I wanted water in me and on me. I gulped down all I could hold and emptied several bottles over my head.

I was in Texas for seven days. The roads were good and the people were even better. They showed great interest in me and what I was trying to do. I can't think of another state where the people have been so cordial and concerned about my welfare. I will never again say bad things about a Texan. The roads displayed all sorts of treasures—enough lost wrenches and other tools to start a hardware store. Present also were dead snakes and armadillos. Bodies of the latter were amalgamated into the paving to produce a surface sometimes better than the original, which now and then exposed large sharp aggregate.

Every night I stayed in a motel and called Anne. She had requested a daily report on my progress. I hate to do this, because even on the best of trips you have some downer days. It is difficult for me to disguise my attitude, even over the telephone. In closing our conversation I would confess, "This is really a dumb thing I am doing."

"You are doing good," she would say, trying to jack me up. "A lot of people here are pulling for you."

The primary deterrent to camping out was my desire to shower and doctor my sore rear. Wind and snow had made training rides impossible before I left Denver and I was paying the price. Otherwise, things were going moderately well. The winds abated, the country greened, I was eating up the miles, the folks were all friendly. I played games with a donkey, a dog, and a turtle. The shelled one had decided to cross the highway and I realized he did not have a chance of making it without instant flattening by a car or truck. I stopped to render assistance. He retreated into his house but came out after a few minutes to discover that he was on the other side of the asphalt.

Things started to go sour east of Texarcana. I was admiring the pretty trees in a misty light while crossing a concrete bridge with massive monolithic railings. I happened to look up and saw a log truck coming straight at me on my side of the road. I had nowhere to escape. The truck also was committed, passing another vehicle. The trucker and I both rode it through. I don't know who was scared the most. I briefly glimpsed his face when he roared by. He was wide eyed.

There was absolutely no shoulder south of the Louisiana state line. The white line was painted right at the paving edge. I was to learn that there is very little rideable shoulder in any state east of there. Log trucks were abundant. Another trucker chose to pass a slow farm vehicle coming toward me. I left the road at high speed, onto the gravel to avoid a head-on. At Hodge, Louisiana, there is a huge paper mill. North of the town are two long bridges with ruined decks which would jeopardize even an automobile. I ran these bridges as fast as I could pedal, but still could not avoid the log trucks gaining on me. They blared their air horns and expected me to disappear.

The roads in Louisiana were awful. I couldn't get out of the state quickly enough. Not only the truckers, but other drivers were openly hostile. They blared and glared at me. There was no place to take refuge. If I had chosen to leave the road at the approach of each vehicle, I would never have gotten anywhere.

East of Natchez, Mississippi, I welcomed the respite of a four-lane highway. However, I could detect in my mirror cars coming up fast in my lane. They were slow to react, apparently unused to bikers. They seemed to have problems anticipating and making a lane change. It was very unnerving. Then U.S. 98 became a two-lane, and the outright hostility returned. I was very wary, conscious always of the risk, afraid to relax. A string of eight semi's passed me, each one crowding me closer as he went by. I left the road after the fifth truck brushed by and stood by my bike to salute the remaining three. I could imagine the conversation on their CB's. At least the road surfaces in Mississippi were an improvement over those in Louisiana.

Near Smithdale the clouds dumped on me. I took refuge from the downpour in a tiny barn and put on more clothes. Water flowed in on the floor leaving me little room to stand in the dry. When I looked out through cracks between the wooden siding, it appeared that the storm was passing over. I carried the bike out to the road and got on. I traveled about one-quarter mile and was pounded again. There was a small store ahead. I slid to a halt, leaned my bike against a wall, and burst in.

"Could I bring my bike in out of the rain?" I asked. Then, as an afterthought, "It's only a bicycle."

"I'd rather you didn't," the lady said. "We have no floor drains and I have trouble cleaning up the water."

I turned to find a shelter for my bike, away from the rain sheets under the eaves. The lady appeared at another door. "Bring it in here," she said.

I spent over an hour talking to Patsy Townsend. She was interested in my adventures and told me how to get to McComb on 570, without the heavy traffic on U.S. 98. While we were talking, the gale blew open her front door and flooded the place anyway.

The rain had almost quit when I reached McComb, about twenty miles away, but I kept my orange jacket on to be visible. A car cut in front of me to enter a drive-in restaurant. I jumped on the brakes, turned sharply, and fought to stay upright. I yelled through all this, which made the driver stop. I came alongside.

"Did you hit me?" he asked.

"No."

"Then what's the problem?"

"Did you see me at all?"

"No."

"That's the problem."

I was happy to ride into Mobile. I felt safer in the city, for once, than on the highways. Maybe it's because it was Sunday and traffic was light. I was trying to find a Best Western Motel near the battleship Alabama, so I could tour the vessel the next day. However, there was a serious obstacle. The highway went through a tunnel where bikes were not allowed. I went to a nearby police station and asked what to do.

"I dunno. Guess you'll just have to somehow find a ride in a car or truck," an officer told me.

I stationed myself next to the ramp, holding the bike, and stuck out my thumb. The first pickup to approach pulled over and stopped. A man got out. He understood my dilemma. His name was Joe Brown.

"Does your tailgate open?" I asked. "This thing weighs about seventy pounds." He lowered the gate, I heaved the bike in and climbed in after it. Joe raced his truck through the tunnel. The speed in the enclosed space frightened me. He stopped at the other end, got out and yelled at me above the traffic din.

"There is a bridge here which also could be a problem for you. Where exactly are you headed?"

"I'm trying to find a Best Western near the Alabama," I shouted.

"Hang on. I'll take you right there."

I thanked Joe profusely, but I guess he was non-plussed by the whole routine.

"My kids ride their bikes through the tunnel all the time, just for the hell of it," he stated. That might be a real kick on an empty racer, but I had survived enough thrills for one day.

Then I had a ball. I went on three self-guided tours of BB 60, the *Alabama,* following colored arrows and numbers through its innards. The gray paint and cramped quarters on this huge old ship had overtones of a prison, but the technology was fascinating. A trip through the submarine USS *Drum* made me even more claustrophobic. I admired aircraft on display nearby and spent several minutes studying a heavily armed F4U. I could hear in my mind the scream of its engine. When I closed my eyes, I could hear and see the *Corsair* rounding a pylon at the Reno Air Races. It did not have a chance of catching the P-51's, but if there had been a prize for noise, the checker-cowled F4U would have won hands down. When wound up, the *Corsair* makes a very distinctive sound. I believe the Japanese called it "Whistling Death." I learned the reason for the cant in the *Corsair's* wings. The prop is so huge that the designers opted for inverted gull wings to provide clearance from the ground. It was either that or mount long unstable landing gear below a conventional wing.

At about noon I headed toward Pensacola by way of Point Clear. A gent at the motel had encouraged me to take the scenic route. The mansions looked posh but I could never see the ocean. I stayed in a pretty grungy motel very near the entrance to the Naval Air Station. I think my quarters were intended for quick trysts.

Military policemen at the gate kindly oversaw my equipment while I hitched a ride to the U.S. Naval Aviation Museum. It is the finest facility of that sort which I have visited, surpassing even the Smithsonian's Air and Space building. The airplanes are immaculate. I photographed models, memorabilia, planes, and paintings. I discovered a Douglas *Dauntless* SBD which had been flown by a crewmate of a fraternity brother. It had "Lt. Cook Cleland USNR" stenciled below the cockpit. I carefully crept over the barrier for a close photo. I was chagrined to learn that their *Yellow Peril* was a float plane, not the Stearman PT-13 I had flown. I could have spent days in the museum but after about two hours I caught another ride back to my bike, in an eighteen-wheeler tractor, of all things. Dick, the driver, worked for the Timken Bearing Company in Cleveland. I gathered that he did not normally drive trucks, but had a more responsible position with the company. He was very friendly and interested in my bike trip. I was impressed by all the modern paraphernalia in his cab. The secure habitat of a truck driver is little akin to that of a cyclist.

Then I pedaled through downtown Pensacola onto a causeway across the bay. It was a four-lane, with the two west lanes under repair. Before it dawned on me that I could have ridden the west lanes anyway, I was committed in heavy two-way traffic, riding tight to a concrete barrier for about five miles. One false move and I would have been scrubbed.

A second bridge took me to Pensacola Beach on Santa Rosa Island. I lunched on two bottles of beer and a strange dozen fresh oysters, stripped from their shells before my eyes. There were fourteen of them. Oysters, not eyes.

Heading east on 399 I rode through sand dune country as I appraised the beachfront architecture. A quick turn onto a boardwalk rewarded me with a close visit to the Gulf where bathers politely used my camera to take a picture of me, for a change. There was no traffic at all on 399 and I was really having a good time. Then a car sped by and the passenger screamed at me. This is unnerving for a biker, even if he is experienced on the road. The car turned in at a parking lot about a half mile ahead, so I decided to follow. I came up on the driver's side. He was astonished to see me ride up as he got out. Then I rode around his hood to address the aggravating passenger.

"What's up?" he asked.

"I thought I should meet you," I replied. "I just wondered what one of you loud jokers looked like."

"I was only showing a little exuberance."

"Your exuberance is rude and dangerous."

"I'll be more selective the next time I choose to kick ass."

"You haven't kicked any, yet."

He swore at me, but turned away. I rode away smiling, pleased that for once I had chosen the proper words.

When I entered U.S. 98 again at Navarre, the traffic got to me immediately. My original intent was to go farther east, but it was not worth the trauma. I went north from Fort Walton Beach through the huge acreage of Eglin Air Force Base and into Alabama again. I had my first flat. I decided to pull both wheels in order to rotate tires. The back one, as usual, was balding. In Florala, I stopped for lunch. A nice little old granny came over to my table and sat down with me to help me choose from her handwritten menu on the wall. She was a sweety.

I called Joy Kendall from my motel in Luverne. "I think it will take me three more days to reach Chattanooga," I said.

"That would be Saturday, right? We have a function to attend until 9:00 that evening. On Sunday, we have to leave town to pick up our daughter."

"I will call you tomorrow night to tell you how I'm doing," I said. After I hung up, I realized that I had to make a decision and I had to make it before I started the next morning. It looked like chancy work to ride to Chattanooga to visit people whom I did not know, and who had other commitments. The smart move was probably to head east into Georgia, saving me at least one hundred miles. That's what I decided to do. I found a *super* bike road, 223 east of Troy. But it only lasted for about twenty-five miles. It took me to Union Springs, where I stoked up on good home-cooked food in a restaurant run by blacks. The roads and people in Alabama had been pretty good to me. I was only having two or three scares a day.

Then I turned onto U.S. 431 at Seale and was confronted by seventeen miles of sheer treachery. Irate drivers, in both cars and trucks, were passing way too close. I pulled off twice, but the traffic near day end only increased, and I had to get to Columbus. The last five miles would change to four-lane, so I pressed on. An angry semi driver gave me air as I entered the refuge of the multiple highway. I stabbed hard with my left hand, signalling for him to move out into the other lane. He had plenty of room. There were no other vehicles around. He pulled out, for awhile. Then he turned back in on me and his trailer missed me by inches. It had to be deliberate.

The next day, while I was stumbling northeast through Georgia, I had my second flat right in Concord. I replaced the tube and entered a restaurant for lunch. Folks there told me to go talk to John Strickland, another biker type, who runs the general store. Reluctantly, I ambled over there, just to appease everyone. He really helped me, put me on roads which would work for my grand plan and were fairly free of traffic. Only one ready mix driver took exception to my presence. I got to McDonough in mid-afternoon, so decided to attempt the ride to Covington, even though the sky was black. About four miles out, I was drenched. I made a 180, but could hardly move into the wind. There was an open garage at a house nearby, so I headed into it. The rain lessened, so I pushed on to Covington. My panniers were full of water that night. I emptied all of the bags and tried to dry things out. My computer was not behaving. It was upset by the moisture. I monkeyed with it and inadvertently scrubbed the numbers indicating total miles traveled. I did not discover until the next day that the device also needed to be recalibrated. I could not remember how. That would take a phone call to Anne, probably two, so she could search for the directions.

I think it was Commerce where I entered a police station to get road advice. Two officers came into the hallway to talk to me.

"It looks to me like I'm faced with about four miles of interstate in order to enter South Carolina," I said.

"You got it. It's the only way unless you head up to Toccoa, and that means mountains," one said.

"It's also farther," said the other.

"I'm not supposed to ride on an interstate."

"I'd go for it if I were you. The highway patrol in North Carolina is not as lenient as ours, but chances are you can get through there without being seen."

With that sound advice, I planned to stay on the little road I had chosen until it petered out, just south of the interstate. Then, about four miles east of Lavonia, I would sneak over onto the big highway. If caught, I would rely on my charming manner and cite the counsel of my uniformed friends in Georgia. It was interesting to me that peace officers here were sensitive to my plight, not taking a hard-line position.

The only trouble with my scheme was that my derailleur in back failed after about ten miles. It would not throw to the rear and keep the chain taut. It appeared that a spring was broken, so I jury-rigged a bungee cord to hold the derailleur in place and with chain almost touching the paving, I fumbled forward. I was reluctant to shift much, afraid that movement might throw the bungee into the spokes, which could be disastrous. So I then cranked the hills in too high a gear, wrecking my knees, and left the saddle when I had to. I wanted to go like blazes on the interstate, but my foray there did not set any records. I needed gears badly.

There are some monster hills south of Seneca so my velocity on that leg was laughable also. I was going as hard as I could to try to get into a bike shop. It was Saturday. I arrived too late to search out repair facilities. I had forewarned a relative, Dr. Dean Dobson, of my approach to Seneca. He and Betty Lou fed me well and we watched two of their kids perform in *The Wizard of Oz* that evening before I turned in. It took my mind off my troubles.

I found a bike shop in Tiger Paw country at Clemson the next morning, but was not surprised that it was closed. I wanted to get close to or in Greenville so that repairs might be made early on Monday. So I rode to Taylors, where Anne corresponded with a college chum, Shirl

Feekin. She and Fred entertained me royally. I was pretty burnt out emotionally by the time I got to their place, so I quickly announced, "I may just stay here forever." They took that in good stride. I don't think they really knew how discouraged I was at that point.

On Monday, Shirl and I stuffed my bike in her car and she drove me to a bike shop. A new derailleur, chain, cable, and cable housing were installed. The shop proprietor was a bit of a clown, so we bantered some while he worked. I told him of my plan to ride north on U.S. 25 for access eventually to the Blue Ridge Parkway.

"You are going to love four miles of thirteen-percent grade," he offered.

"What's that?" I said. "There is no way I can crank a thirteen-percent hill with the load I am carrying." We discussed alternatives. They did not sound good. That night, when Fred came home from work, Shirl and I told him of my concerns. He allowed as how he had some difficulty pulling his trailer up that highway, but he could not remember exactly where. They drove me out north that evening to look at the road, but it got dark and we headed back.

The next morning it was raining—hard. I said to Shirl, "If it's all right with you, I think I would like to stay one more day. This rain looks like it means business."

"That's fine," she said. "Is there any place you would like to go? Anything you would like to see?"

"I would like to see more of Highway 25," I said. She knew I was worrying about it, so she drove me clear to Hendersonville and back by another route, a total of about eighty miles. I carefully studied all the hills through the rainstreaked windshield.

"They look moderately steep," I said, "but I haven't seen anything yet that I think I can't manage." That evening I announced to Fred, "By this time tomorrow I should be camped out on the parkway." He nodded in the affirmative.

The monster hill was there all right, but it was no thirteen percent. It was on the last four miles before the North Carolina state line. I cranked it without a stop. However, the wind from the north increased and it got cold at the higher elevation. I rode by Carl Sandburg's home, but stopped just long enough to snap a photo. I was freezing. I rode into Hendersonville, had lunch, and put on more clothes right in the restaurant in view of all the patrons.

A lady in a visitor's center insisted that I would be better off riding 191 than U.S. 25 toward Asheville. "You'll have a lot less traffic and no trucks at all," she said. "You will cross the Blue Ridge Parkway eighteen miles out." She sounded like she knew her business, so I got on 191. Boy, was that a mistake. The traffic was substantial and there was a plethora of trucks. I passed a sign which tersely stated "parkway" before a road went off to the left. I figured that access to the parkway running east of me would appear at any moment. It never did. I wound through a maze of short little runs on and near controlled access highways. It was misty moisty out and the light was flat. Even without the sun I sensed that I was far west of Highway 25. I did not know that I had a reasonably good detail map of Asheville buried in my panniers. I found a convenience store. There were several people inside, all of whom offered suggestions to get me back on track toward the parkway. The debate aspects of their exhortations to each other did not inspire any confidence. In order to end the dialogue and exit gracefully without insulting someone, I asked if they could direct me to a motel. That was easier for them. I followed their directions along a river but it seemed that I was making way too many turns to the right before I saw a motel in the distance. I entered the motel office, rang a bell, and a woman appeared.

"I haven't the slightest idea where I am," I said. This was a rare admission for me. I do not know why I delivered the confession in that manner.

"You are in an exclusive area adjacent to the Biltmore Estate," she said haughtily. That did not help me one bit.

"I am trying to get on the Blue Ridge Parkway heading northeast." A boy appeared behind her and he started to laugh. He had overheard our conversation.

"If you get on the parkway, you'll go where it takes you, unless you can ride that thing through the trees," he stated mockingly. My patience was worn thin.

"Young man, the parkway heads both southwest from Asheville and northeast from Asheville. In the past few hours I have talked to several folks who cannot comprehend this. You appear to have the same problem. I want to go northeast."

"You'll have to go this way," the lady pointed.

"Which direction is that?" I asked.

"South. It's three miles to the parkway."

"South? You're kidding."

"I'll get a map," she said. I studied the document and realized how hopelessly confused I was. I had ridden far to the west, made a half circle around to the right and was now heading back toward Hendersonville. I had not yet reached Asheville proper.

"Why would you direct me south when it appears that I can enter the parkway by going north, here or here?" I pointed to the map.

"I wouldn't know about that. I send all the tourists south. It's easier for them."

"It may be easier for them in a car, but that's six miles out of my way."

"Maybe you had better talk to my husband. He will be back in about an hour."

"Do you have a vacancy?" I asked. It was only 3:30 but I was done in for the day.

I walked four blocks to a restaurant the next morning through a light drizzle. It was very cold outside and clouds hung close overhead. I talked to the cafe manager about riding the parkway. "You are going to freeze," he said. "The road is close to Mt. Mitchell. I also doubt if you will be able to see anything at all."

Abandoning my plan to ride the Blue Ridge Parkway, I rode north on U.S. 23 toward Tennessee. The hills got tougher and there were two mean long suckers just south of the state line. I stopped in a little grocery and a lady told me the temperature outside was 37 degrees. I was alternately donning and doffing attire. The climbs made me sweat profusely and I was chilled on the downslopes. A big truck approached as I topped the last ridge and discovered Tennessee's welcoming sign. The truck driver gave me a thumbs up, which was a rare occurrence for these parts. I lived on that for the rest of the day.

The little portion of eastern Tennessee which I traveled was delightful. The roads were good and I was able to look around for a change, not constantly wary. I was enjoying the scenery so much that a lone chuckhole escaped my attention and it produced a flat spot on the rear rim. I was annoyed by a thump, thump, thump for all of the remaining miles, in spite of several attempts to round the wheel by adjusting spoke tension. My posterior paid dearly for the pounding.

At a restaurant in Bristol, Tennessee, I asked my waitress, "Could you have these dinner rolls put in a doggy bag? They could save my bacon." She gave me a puzzled look, but returned with a neat package. Two days later I laughed as I withdrew a bacon sandwich from the wrappings.

The roads deteriorated as I rode northward through the point of Virginia, into West Virginia, and turned toward Kentucky. Some of the drivers were angry at my presence, others did not know how to deal with a biker. They would dog me, afraid to pass, requiring eight or ten feet of side clearance before they would maneuver around my bike. A driver who hangs on is a potential hazard to the cyclist, particularly when broken and buckled paving must be negotiated.

Blind right-hand turns on an upgrade can be lethal. A vehicle comes up on a slowly ascending bike without warning to driver or biker. Remember, the rideable shoulder was nonexistent. Escape to a rocky ravine adjacent was not a viable alternative.

I felt hemmed in by the environment, swallowed by thick stands of trees in fog and drizzle. Sight distance for me or a motorist was minimal. The great expansive views to a distant horizon were never present. It was a far cry from cycling in the West.

Why were some of the drivers so paranoid about me? Surely they had to deal on occasion with a cyclist. I knew that the Southeast had some strong tourers and some fine rides. Anne and I offered camping space near Estes Park once to a tourer and his companion from the Southeast. He turned out to be the president of the North Carolina Bicycle Touring Society, Bill Mason. That club, and others like it, must surely create some awareness.

I had been forewarned by several of my friends to be on guard for "rednecks" in the South. I do not know exactly what a redneck is. I did not observe anyone with scarlet skin. One on one, when I could talk to the people they were courteous and friendly, many very interested in my mission or in awe of my equipment. The blacks, I think, were more tolerant of my presence than the whites, perhaps because they sympathized with my minority status. Or maybe they appreciated the simple economy of my conveyance. If I said "Hello" or "Good Morning" to black females as I rode by, they always returned my greeting. The men usually did not, unless I was off the bike, face to face with them. It was only when they got behind a steering wheel that a few southerners went berserk. There are a few fruitcakes everywhere, but it seemed that the nuttiest ones were holding a convention in my vicinity.

There was absolutely no instance of positive communication, verbal or otherwise, from automobiles as they passed me. This is atypical of most tours. A friendly shout or sign boosts a tired traveler. When I am driving our Saab and see a biker with a humongous load, I lightly tap the horn twice *after* clearing him and thrust my hand through the sunroof in a thumbs up. He invariably waves back after quickly reading the exhortation on our license plates, a full sentence stating "BIKE

Colorado." (The plates were a birthday present from my kids. I don't think the youngsters knew that I would be honored with a twenty-five-dollar additional fee each subsequent year. Is this a gift that keeps on giving, or what?)

You have probably gathered by now that I am not totally adverse to dealing with some risk. But this tour was ridiculous. It ceased to be fun very soon after I entered Arkansas. Every night I was totally drained by the day's activity. It was not the riding which left me spent. The ride was no big deal. I was a wreck from being on guard all day, trying to protect myself, and wanted to end the ordeal as quickly as possible.

I did not know it at the time, but there was an unopened letter waiting for me at home, sent from the state of Oregon. It would later inform me that the insurance company carrying my major medical coverage was defunct, dead, bankrupt. I was unknowingly struggling through the Southeast without any chance of help from my insurer. But I, not with clairvoyance but rather suspicions about previous correspondence, had taken my business elsewhere, relying on a better Protector.

Every morning I said a prayer before I got on the road. It would go something like this: "Lord, you got me through another day and I thank you for that. I am very sorry to have gotten us into this mess, but I really feel obligated to try to finish it. If you can see your way clear to hang with me for another day, I would really appreciate it. If something happens to me, it's going to be a big hassle for Anne. I am trying to stay alert. Please deal with the things that I cannot control as you see best. Amen." Anne told me after the tour that some of the people in our church had me on a prayer chain. I guess I should have known that. Something was working. The things I was doing and saying were not the best.

This will at first appear to be very immodest, but I do not know personally any other cyclist who would have much chance of finishing this tour. I know a bunch of super macho tough bikers, but they are almost too free-spirited to make this particular ride. They are used to all fun stuff on a bicycle. And they are smarter than I am. They would quickly recognize the strong possibility of being erased somewhere east of Texas and I can hear them saying, "Screw it, Bob, it isn't worth the effort. I'm outta here." Either that, or they would spend an interminable amount of time searching for alternate routes. If you grant that others have the road experience to recognize the risks, I doubt that they would have the dedication to stay on guard hour after hour, mile after mile. They also would not have the ultimate goal in mind, which possessed me.

I entered Bradshaw, West Virginia, exhausted from a long day of hills, curvy back roads, and thoughtless drivers, I tried to sort out verbal directions from the natives. Some of the advice was good, some bad. Twice I was confronted by tobacco chewers who were more pressed to expectorate than elucidate. It made our conversation less than spontaneous. I was depressed by the poverty in the coal country. I passed hovels on ground littered with trash. Debris was in the ditches. Trees by the rivers were draped with strings of garbage, relocated downstream by a flood stage current. The people were dirty and unkempt, many sooted by coal dust. Poverty and filth had etched a gray shroud on the land and the people. I asked about a motel, which I had been assured by Virginians, existed in Bradshaw. Now I was told, "There ain't any. There ain't nuthin' in this dump."

I rode on toward Iaeger, my eyes searching the roadside for a reasonably clean and secure campsite. Nothing looked very inviting. In Iaeger I inquired at a grocery about camping facilities. The people there were no help. I went to a school and asked if I could camp on their grounds and was told the principal would have to rule on that and he had gone home. Three young boys suggested that I climb up a steep gravel road to a clifftop site. That had no appeal. They were very interested in where I was going to locate for the night—too interested. I went into a service station where four people were gathered. "Do you know of anyone who would allow me to set up a tent on their property?" I asked. They all shook their heads and just stared at me. I walked across the room to a pay phone, dropped in some coins, and dialed. I heard Anne come on the line.

"Collect from Bob," the operator said. "Will you pay?"

"Sure," said Anne.

"I'm in Iaeger, West Virginia. That's I-A-E-G-E-R. I've come 113 miles and I'm pretty strung out. There are no motels near here and I'll have to camp out. It will probably be somewhere north on 52. There are no campgrounds. I love you. Goodbye." The people were still staring at me, listening.

"You could at least get your three minute's worth," Anne said.

"No I can't. I'll explain later." I hung up.

When I walked outside a young man followed me. "You can camp out at my place," he said. "It's not much but you are welcome. It's about a mile from here. I can take you out in my truck." My ploy was successful. Michael Adair drove me to his home and I set up my tent by a gurgling little stream, stripped the bike of its bags, and crawled in to prepare dinner. I was too tired to be polite and converse with my host.

Coal trucks drove by into the night but I did not hear them for long.

It was a half circle from there into Kentucky. West of Pikeville, I stopped at a state highway patrol office on a Sunday morning. Two officers were present.

"Can I ride the Bert T. Combs Mountain Parkway?" I asked.

"Sure. If you're going west that would be your easiest route. There's only one tough hill. You'll probably have to walk it."

"Thank you."

"Be careful."

"I am making a career of that."

When I came to the parkway entrance, a sign advised me "No Bicycles." I rode it anyway, for the full length. The hills were all moderate, the patrolman's assessment of grade or my ability totally incorrect. The parkway changed to a four-lane and dumped me on Interstate 64, which I rode for about a mile to Winchester. The next day I rode through Lexington on U.S. 60 and through lovely horse-farm country which had magnificent estates surrounded by carefully laid loose stone walls or creosoted fences. Coming up a hill leaving Frankfort, I saw a potential problem ahead. I was right next to the capital building on a four-lane, no shoulder. A police car had stopped someone in the right lane and beyond them was a blind curve to the right. I was not concerned about getting around the parked vehicles. I could do that in an instant. I was worried about the aftermath. What do you do when you drive past an emergency vehicle parked on the road? You look in your mirror to check out the situation, right? I passed the cars and was straining around the curve when I heard the scream of skidding tires behind me. The distracted driver barely managed to get his car slowed and under control before he snuffed me.

I spent a night at the home of Doris and Dale Detlefs in Louisville. The tour was over. I had ridden 2,648 miles—away from home for a month but riding only 26½ days. It was too bad that I did not tool around Louisville for two more miles, in order to lay claim to a precise one-hundred-mile per day average. Doris took me and my bike to a shop where they dismantled my faithful companion and packed it in a box for shipping. Then she took me, the box, and my assembly of bags to a bus depot. I spent a sleepless night riding a succession of three different buses to St. Louis and then north to Mount Pleasant, Iowa. During the daylight hours on the bus, I totally enjoyed streaking past the big trucks. I could look right into the cabs at the drivers. I tactfully avoided delivering a salute.

In Mt. Pleasant I could not get a cab or rent a car, so I reassembled the bike, hung all the bags on it, and rode about a mile north of town to search out a motel. I had lunch and rode back into town on the empty bike. I visited the public library, the county courthouse, and two cemeteries. I carefully explained to the librarians, "My wife is the genealogical whiz, but she won't be here until tomorrow, I think. If I can just do something worth while here in the way of research, she will be very proud of me." They laughed and dug out tattered old documents. I walked through one cemetery in a careful systematic search, but the grave markers were all very old, mostly illegible, and I was discouraged because I was on the last row. Then I saw the stone. It read "Chas. Voiland." I had found the graves of my great grandfather and some of his family.

Late that afternoon I showered and poured myself a toddy. I was standing naked in the motel room when there was a knock on the door. I cracked it open and peered out. It was Anne, my rescuer. She entered the room and we embraced. I was so happy to see her that I almost cried. Then I turned to get dressed and she said, "Your rear end is all black and blue."

It's all over. I did all the forty-eight states, from Denver, what I set out to do. Some days I think, "What a dumb thing. You crazy dope. All those miles, all that hurt. You strung yourself out like laundry, just asking to get blown away. You gave up a half year of your life to pedal around on that silly machine. Who cares? Why did you bother?" Other days I think, "YOU DID IT. YOU DID IT."

I did not make a point of counting other bikers on the trip to the Southeast, but I probably passed a dozen, at the most. Half were kids on a fat-tired Huffy. The other half were probably riding Highway 399 near Pensacola Beach. I met one loaded tourer in Vidalia, Louisiana. I think he had ridden from Jacksonville. He deserves credit for getting through Florida alive. Shortly after my tour, Anne and I drove from our house in Lakewood to Estes Park on a Saturday morning of the Memorial Day weekend. Lots of traffic. I counted 30 bikers between Lakewood and Boulder, 51 from Boulder to Lyons, and 7 on the deceptively tough pitches west of Lyons. That's 88 bikers in 64 miles. Colorado motorists may not be unanimous in their respect for cyclists, but they have had to learn how to cope with them. You wonder why I prefer to ride in the West?

CHAPTER 18

NAVIGATION

Bob McNeill and I had completed a successful elk hunt. We had not found our quarry but did delight in the sanctity of the forest, marred only by an unusual number of aircraft flyovers. On our second evening in a cabin near Hahns Peak we were preparing dinner when interrupted by a knock at the door. A worried-looking young man entered. "I'm looking for my brother," he said. "He is somewhere in the area, but we can't find his camp or vehicle. Without a lead, we don't know where to start searching. He has a heart problem." That explained the airplanes.

Now, three days later, McNeill and I were loading the jeep, ready to head home. A car drove up and a game warden asked us to start searching for the lost hunter. "We would appreciate some quick help from you boys. You are the only ones close with snowshoes. We just found his vehicle. It's only a couple of miles down the highway, hidden back in the trees." McNeill and I grabbed our rifles, got ammo, candy bars, and canteen out of our luggage. We followed the warden's car in our own machine to a clearing by the paving. I could barely make out a jeep through the tree limbs. It was hidden by its own green. The warden motioned to me, "If you can get on these tracks here, I'll lead your friend down the road a ways. I've another idea for him to pursue." They left me as I strapped on my trail shoes, each fifty-six inches long by ten inches wide.

It was fortunate that I had the snowshoes, although the snow was hardly deep enough to require their use. The tracks I was following were a copy of my own, the right footprint splayed outward at an angle more severely than the left. When the tracks milled around in a stand of timber, it was difficult to find where the hunter made his exit to press onward. Without the snowshoes, I might have tracked myself.

I walked for maybe a mile and a half, following my nose, conscious of a plane circling above me. It was trying to keep track of me as I followed the telltale prints in and out of the meadows and gentle wooded slopes. In the open parks, the tracks looked very old, much ravaged by the sun. At a very long meadow, I saw McNeill far in the distance coming toward me. He waved. Then, at about the same instant, we both quickened our pace as we saw a dark object in the snow about half way between us.

A frozen human body is not a pleasant sight. I turned away quickly and sought an expanse of snow where I could "write" a message. I stomped out three large letters, D E D. My eyes misted as the plane made a final pass, waggling its wings. McNeill had entered the valley from another access road, pointed toward an abandoned cabin where he discovered the peculiar splayed tracks floundering in and out of the structure. He also found broad imprints where the hunter had fallen. It was obvious to McNeill that the hunter had been in great distress, his heart failing from the uncommon exertion. McNeill reasoned that the hunter must have lain in the cabin for a time and then attempted to backtrack out.

I was astonished at the quick arrival of officials, who drove their four-wheel-drive vehicles through the snow to a point within fifty yards of the body. We were parallel to the highway and only a short distance from it. Neither I nor the dead hunter had any notion that help was so close at hand. It is always nice to know where you are.

On another occasion, I had walked many miles near the Sanchez Lakes, looking for the wily wapiti in the Mount Zirkle Wilderness Area. Nightfall was approaching and nothing around me looked familiar. I hurried on, starting to sweat from the physical effort and growing panic. I was violating the survival rules to sit down, collect your wits, gather dry wood, start a warm fire, and get as comfortable as possible. I was reluctant to spend a night out in the forest. It was total darkness when I saw the light from a tent. When I entered the sanctuary and was offered a hot cup of coffee, a lone sportsman said, "You are not far from your camp. I passed it down on the ridge as I drove in. Couldn't be more than a mile." I thanked him, gulped the coffee, and prepared to leave. "Would you like to borrow a flashlight?" he asked. I declined, too proud and too hurried. I stepped out into the inky night and marched away. He stood in the parted canopy of the doorway and watched me. I heard a yell. "Hey," he shouted. You are headed right back the way you came."

"Oh yeah, gotcha," I called.

"You sure you don't want a flashlight?"

"No. I'm O.K."

I had to light a match several times, holding it down by my feet so I could examine the ground for some trace of a deep track. It was not much of a road. When I finally entered my own tent, my companions were enjoying the cocktail hour, not yet concerned by my absence. "We knew you would be in soon," one said. At that hour they had more confidence than I did. I told them a bit about my blunders, but I did not tell them everything.

Anne says I have a good sense of direction and I guess that is usually true. I am somewhat like Daniel Boone, who is purported to have said, "I have never been lost, but I was confused once for three days."

The World War II Navy pilots had a reputation for being the worst navigators in the world. Army pilots at that time (there was no Air Force) jokingly warned each other, "Never try to find your way by following a railroad track. You'll crash into a Navy plane." When I was in V5 at Swarthmore, we had a beginner's course in navigation. Most of my fellow students, future pilot material, were awful at applying the fundamentals. We were all given plastic plotting boards to hold in our lap, spinning a wheel in order to solve problems concerning flights from a moving aircraft carrier. These were simple vector problems in dead reckoning. The lack of skill apparent among my fellow sailors made the "dead" description very appropriate. I was not stellar at navigation, but I got a "B" in the course. During the exams, my friends had a few of the math whizzes (me included) sit in strategic scattered locations of the classroom amphitheater. They hoped to watch us turn the plastic wheel and copy our lead. I don't think it helped.

During my short stay in Memphis, our base was invited to participate in a nationwide Navy swimming meet at Jacksonville. I was asked to join the team because I was the only one on the whole air station who could swim anything resembling the butterfly. It was a lark to fly down to Florida in a C47 for this event. There were hotshot swimmers competing, including Johnny Higgins, former olympic breaststroke competitor. He was coach of the team of cadets from Ottumwa. Although coaches could enter any event, Johnny chose to swim the backstroke, which he won. His cadets took the butterfly handily, first, second, and third. I came in second in my heat, but did not qualify for the finals—time too slow.

Our team flew back to Memphis rather discouraged, even though two divers had placed in the meet. Toward the end of our flight we heard an announcement through the aircraft that our Navy pilot was lost and he requested all aboard to look out a window in search of a familiar landmark so he could zero in on Memphis. I do not know if he was serious, but he sure got our attention.

When I returned to college at Iowa State I joined a fraternity. One of the actives was Jim Seybert, a former Navy fighter pilot. Sy never said much about his adventures in the service. One day he approached me, "Some of us are having a little party at my place Saturday night. Do you like applejack? I have found a recipe for a marvelous concoction which combines the brandy with egg yolks. It's called a 'Golden Glow.'"

"I have never tasted applejack, but I'll be there."

During the weekend revelry, our host was chagrined by the huge accumulation of leftover egg whites. Quick reference to his mixology manual produced a drink called an "Apple Blow Fizz" from the available ingredients.

While my friends were glowing and fizzing and joyfully embalming themselves, I cornered Sy's wife, "Sy seems to be reticent about his flying experiences," I said. "I wish he would open up."

"Just a moment," she said, and left the room. She returned with a little book, which she handed to me. It was *Mission Beyond Darkness* by Bryan and Reed. It documented an air strike from the Lexington and other carriers during the First Battle of the Philippines. It detailed a desperate effort to catch a portion of the Japanese Navy which was at extreme range for our dive bombers and torpedo planes. The return from the attack, at night, was for most of the fliers more grim than the battle. Planes were low on fuel and the pilots were unsure of the way home. Some elected to ditch together in the sea to increase their odds for survival. They figured that their task force had a better chance of finding them than they had of locating it. Sy mentally averaged recommended courses gleaned from his radio. Many of the pilots were inexperienced at night landings, some had never made one. Vice-Admiral Marc Mitscher elected to turn on lights, exposing his entire fleet to submarine or air attack, in order to retrieve his pilots. A melee of returning aircraft crowded the "groove" of each carrier, trying to get aboard a deck, any deck. They were consistently waved off until they came in singly. Many, out of gas, crashed in the ocean adjacent to their own ships. Some augured into planes already landed on the flight deck, fouling it for others until the debris could be shoved overboard. Sy took five approaches to get safely aboard his ship.

It occurred to me after reading this account that Sy had been reluctant to relate his experience because he was not very proud of his performance. He and his wingman, plus several other fighter pilots, never found the main engagement. The SBD's and TBM's which they were supposed to protect had to go the battle alone. Sy need not have been shy about his efforts. He was awarded a gold star, in lieu of a second Air Medal.

A bicycle tour is supposed to be devoid of combat. Some hazards are beyond a biker's control, but poor planning or execution can direct his destiny toward a life-threatening situation. A friend of mine, George Shaw, who is a general contractor and sometimes pilot, looks with disdain on any kind of ground travel because it only involves decisions related to two dimensions. Not so for a biker, George, we have to think also about the vertical—about the passes particularly. They can do you in from anoxia, hypothermia, dehydration, or exhaustion.

There are two schools of thought on attacking a pass. Some folks would rather not know about what lies ahead. I would prefer to have some knowledge about the challenge. Awareness of the maximum elevation to be attained helps, but a ride up in a car provides even better information. Slumgullion and Cucharas in Colorado are examples of passes lying hidden, ready to eat you alive. Others announce their presence from afar, producing trepidation in the biker when he looks high into the mountains at an intimidating scar. The view of Independence from the east, Wolf Creek from the south, and Trail Ridge from any direction can dampen one's ardor.

Good maps are helpful when planning a trip, essential while traveling. I used to make photocopies of published maps to insert in my handlebar bag. I don't make copies any more. The full color treatment on the original is too valuable. I dismember an atlas and carry all the necessary pages. The maps have all sorts of information on them: size and quantity of roads, road numbers, mileages, campground and rest stop locations, scenic spots, and more information about the type of terrain than is at first obvious. If rivers cross your route, you can bet on a hilly ride. If the watercourses are parallel to the road, chances are your work will be easier. Look at the layout of the Finger Lakes in western New York State. Is it any wonder that riding U.S. 20 is such a bitch? Look at a map of Colorado and a detail map of Rocky Mountain National Park. That speckled light green indicates forest. To you as a biker it means tough stuff. There are four primary roads to Estes Park, which is quickly seen to be in country elevated above the plains. None of the four are a piece of cake, but U.S. 34 from Loveland, adjacent to the Big Thompson River, is the easiest. Next is U.S. 36 from the southeast. It crosses the Little Thompson River, which would indicate a climb out of Lyons, a drop, then another climb. Actually, there is one more big drop into the Estes valley. From the south, Highways 72 and 7 cross several drainages. You are on a roller coaster. From the west, U.S. 34 is Trail Ridge Road. If the words "closed in winter" do not impress you, the elevations printed nearby should. I have found relief maps in the World Book Encyclopedia to be helpful in spotting trouble routes through a specific state. The highway layouts, in our old set of books at least, are not up to date.

I cannot now imagine touring without an odometer, but I did it for years. On many roads are mileage markers from which you can calculate how far you have gone and what distance remains ahead. Be wary of the markers in states where the numbering restarts at each county line. Those digits may help the road crews, but they can foul up your arithmetic. When you cross a county line, which is usually identified by a sign, be sure to match it with a green line on your map to see exactly where you are. If you have an emergency, you then know the shortest distance to salvation. Be sure to stop at all the historic markers. You might learn something. In the West, you will find that Lewis and Clark unknowingly came near to what are now excellent bike roads. The West is in some ways easier to negotiate than the East, at least on the highways. You don't have as many choices. You can see where you are.

I never thought about it much, until I read a very special magazine ad, but on first examination good vision seems essential for riding a bike. You need to see and interpret the signs, the roadway, the traffic. The ad I saw was a poignant plea from a blind female for a tour companion on a tandem bicycle. She would be the stoker. I wish her well in her quest. I am not sure that I could tolerate the responsibility of acting as pilot on a stretched bike, whether or not the other party had all their faculties. Sometimes I can barely take care of myself. Actually, neither position on a tandem appeals to me, because of the accountability up front or the boredom in back.

If you were in command of a torpedo plane, could you shirk on your navigation homework knowing that a radioman and gunner were counting on your skill? I believe George Bush, former pilot of an aircraft and of a nation, would know what I am getting at. For that matter, an automobile driver can have the same kind of burden. Think about it the next time you have the family out for a drive.

Maps will not tell you about gooey asphalt, detours, shortcuts, motels, and restaurants. Signs can inform you about the first two, but then the warning is too late. This is where the locals can help. Sound guidance from residents has saved me miles of agony. Many a delightful evening has resulted from a friendly suggestion. Take some advice with a grain of salt, however. If the plan seems hokey to you, do not hesitate to secretly verify one person's nifty idea with the opinion of another. Be aware that most people think in terms of auto travel and they think in round numbers. If they tell you it is twenty miles to a campground, it might be fourteen, or thirty. If they tell you it is eighteen miles, it is probably eighteen. I never encountered before so many people eager to give me counsel as I did on my trip to the Southeast. Unfortunately, much of their advice was wrong. Part of the fun of a trip is meeting people, studying their personalities, and enjoying their humor. Now and then you will be betrayed by their lack of wisdom, or yours. Maybe you should approach all strangers with, "Pardon me, would you mind taking a little written test I have developed to evaluate your travel experience? I would rather receive NO advice at all than bad advice." Smooth.

At a motel north of I-20 near Covington, Georgia, I asked a lady at the desk for the best route north to Monroe. She pointed to a little road on a side hill.

"You follow that and it eventually turns and will take you there," she said.

"Won't that put me awfully far west?" I asked.

"Well, I don't know. We take that way all the time. It's a nice road. Maybe you should talk to Harold. He's real good with directions." Now Harold is sitting there beside the desk and he is obligated to perform.

"I'd go back to the main highway south of the interstate," Harold offers.

"Isn't that back a couple of miles?" I hate to backtrack.

"Yep."

I crossed the street to have breakfast and noticed three men talking beside a pickup. Their gun rack was full and they were wearing camouflage clothing. Surely they would know the road layout.

"What's the best and quickest road for me to bicycle to Monroe?" I asked.

"You're standing on it."

I ate my meal and returned to the motel office to pay my bill. "By the way, some hunters across the street told me that the best route to Monroe is to just follow this road that runs in front of your motel," I said.

"Could be. We have never driven there on this road."

"How long have you lived here?"

"Twelve years."

CHAPTER 19

1990—A SMASHING YEAR

In the summer of 1989, I purposely missed the first annual Ride Around Wyoming with its zany T-shirts which admonished "I rode in the RAW." I was suffering from bicycle burnout, a product of the tour to the southeast U.S. By the following winter, I had a more positive outlook. "This Wyoming ride sounds like a kick," I said to Anne. "But I have never been on Ride the Rockies. Maybe I should try for that instead."

"Why don't you do both?" she asked. "Isn't one right after the other?" There was an idea. I could drive from the Wyoming ride direct to Craig, Colorado, for a double dose of touring. Anne volunteered to take a bus to Craig to retrieve my car while I was cranking across the mountains with 1,999 other cyclists. It was not to be. I had no trouble signing up for the Wyoming tour of two hundred people, but the lottery to limit applicants for the Colorado ride returned my entry fee. I was disappointed, even rankled by the rejection, but it turned out to be a blessing.

Filled with resolve to be ready for the Wyoming excursion, I agreed to plan and lead an early Spring one-day ride for the Denver Bicycle Touring Club. It was to be a fifty-miler from Wheat Ridge to Boulder and back. On each leg, we would cover a portion of the Morgul-Bismarck, a favorite training ground for Boulder cyclists. The Morgul-Bismarck, which sounds like an epic conflict between battleships, was actually named for two cats. It is a punishing hilly fourteen-mile circuit between Rocky Flats and Boulder. During the days of the Coors Classic, the men racers rode seven times around this brute, the women four. Two hills are named the Hump and the Wall. The film *Breaking Away* showed the latter, where the start/finish is located, but no movie or photograph can adequately depict the aspects of this climb which destroy mind and body. The Wall is only a half mile long, but the inclination of the roadway gradually increases before it finally crests, testing even the power of an automobile. I have watched racers collapse at the conclusion. I saw one winner waver and fall *before* the finish, pick up his bike and carry it across the line, and *then* collapse. One circuit around the Morgul is enough for me.

At a parking lot in Wheat Ridge, I handed out maps to about thirty riders and had them sign a roster which provided information for the club plus an executed release from liability for any mishap. The D.B.T.C. had learned a bitter lesson from the Colorado Mountain Club, an organization primarily for climbers and hikers, which was almost destroyed by a lawsuit from an unhappy camper. I assigned a point rider whom I knew to be strong and announced that I would follow the pack, for the start at least. My experience is that the leader can best do his job from the tail end position, where one can best identify and deal with a rider problem. The "leader" in that spot can also warn others of an impending threat from other vehicles, hopefully.

I followed along happily, talking to two young men on mountain bikes who were having trouble matching the pace. The rest of our riders were gradually strung out for blocks, which invariably happens as each person settles in to a speed at his comfort level. This stretched spacing of bicyclists, sometimes annoying to motorists, is actually to a driver's advantage, giving him several opportunities to safely pass. The spacing protects cyclists also. Riders in a cluster, just avoiding each other, tend to wander into the traffic lanes. We rode north on McIntyre Street, then Indiana Street, regrouping at its end which is close to the Morgul and about halfway to Boulder. I had overlooked one thing. The infamous spring winds over Rocky Flats were increasing fiercely, right into our face. Several riders elected to turn back. The mountain bike riders had already done so. I was honored that Annie Lombard, the head tour director of our club, had chosen to join us but I was embarrassed that I did not have a Phillips screwdriver to adjust her front derailleur, which was troubling her. It turned out that she had a small screwdriver, but she could not force the screw to yield. Neither could I. Some hunk with vise-like hand strength made the thing cooperate.

The ride into Boulder was not pleasant, punching into the wind. We reassembled at the Mall and only a few of us decided to have lunch. We ate at a restaurant table outdoors, shivering in the breeze, but able to keep a watchful eye on the bicycles. Seated next to me was Carol Gosline, who divulged that she was not yet a club member and that she was a surgical nurse. I told her that I was laboring on a manuscript which she and fellow workers could use to play "Identify the Doctor." Annie joined us also.

On the way home, I could not keep up with Carol without great effort. All of us except Carol attacked the Hump and the Wall gingerly, nothing like a racer would. Annie and Carol later headed off on their separate ways and when I rolled into our starting point, all cyclists' cars were absent from the parking lot.

My good intentions about gradually training into condition went by the wayside as I became involved with the U.S. Census. It looked to me like a lark to receive money for meeting people, so I applied for an enumerator job and was accepted. Later I was amazed at my own lack of perception—that I would be dealing with some folks too lazy or hostile to mail in their questionnaire. Two blind residents I visited seemed to have the only legitimate excuse for procrastination.

Only one week was available to ready myself for the Wyoming bike venture. The plan was to push harder and harder each day, Sunday through Thursday, rest on Friday, then drive to Sheridan on Saturday. By Thursday I was chugging up Coal Creek Canyon toward Wondervu on a difficult but satisfying ride because I seemed to be getting stronger and could manage the grades in the foothills. I cut south on the Peak-to-Peak Highway and then east through Golden Gate Canyon. That road deposited me on Highway 93 (remember?) leading directly onto the main drag of Golden—Washington Street. I was really bombing down the hill, in the curb lane, when a car passed me on the left and pulled over quickly in front of me to slow down and park. Now this has happened to me a lot and up to then I had been able to deal with the problem, either slow down and stop or turn aside. There was no time to check my mirror for an absence of other cars in the main lane. All I could do was go for the brakes and try to stop. I was almost successful. My bicycle skidded into the right rear of the car and the front wheel collapsed. I went up over the handlebars and struck the auto, then fell back onto the pavement.

People were running toward me. I just sat on the asphalt, dazed. The driver did not exit the car immediately. A lady leaned over me and asked, "Are you all right?"

"I don't know yet."

"I am a nurse. Tell me where you hurt."

"My shoulder." I was rubbing my left shoulder and collarbone, feeling for shattered parts. I found none, but it hurt like hell.

"You're white as a sheet. You'd better sit still."

"I had a scare." Then I stood up, still rubbing my shoulder. I was now visible to the driver and she got out of her car.

"I didn't even see you," she said.

"I know." A patrol car stopped and a policeman walked over.

"Are you injured?" he asked.

"Some," I said.

He asked where and I explained. He volunteered to call an ambulance. I saw dollar signs.

"No way," I said. "I'll get myself to a doctor." Someone offered paper and pencil and I shakily took down names and phone numbers. While the policeman cited the driver, I called Anne from a store adjacent to report my predicament, asking her to pick me up at Self Propulsion, Portia's bike shop. I walked to the shop, supporting the front end of my bike which was a pretzel.

The doctor peered at my x-ray and said, "Nothing is broken. I'd call it a sprain or strain of the A-C joint, hardly any separation. Ice for twenty-four hours, then heat." He handed me a small plastic bottle and added, "Try these."

"What are they?"

"An anti-inflammatory medication."

"I've tried that kind of stuff for the tendinitis. It tears up my guts."

"These are new. Just try them. And another thing, you shouldn't be on a bike again for six weeks."

"Aw, come on. I have a tour in Wyoming in two days. I've looked forward to it for over a year."

He watched me try to get my shirt back on. I could hardly get my left arm over my head. "Come in Saturday and we'll see how you are," he said.

"Can it be early? I was planning to drive to Sheridan on Saturday."

Portia's people didn't have a matching front wheel for my bike, but they had a rim that was reasonable, so they built a wheel for me in one day, attaching new spokes to my old hub. There was no frame damage. I picked up the bike in my car, thanked them for the speedy service, and drove home. Then I gingerly tested everything in my driveway. It was mostly to check out me, not the bike. It actually felt better to have my arms supported up on the handlebars than to have them hanging at my sides. I knew that if I passed on the tour, standing around like a sullen goon, that I would never forgive myself. It was important to get back on the horse. I lounged under an ice pack for the rest of the day and switched to a heating pad that night. My damaged front rim was displayed in a conspicuous position in our garage, to keep me humble.

Saturday came. I dutifully visited the doctor to exhibit the renewed mobility in my left arm, got in the car and headed for Wyoming. My intent was to camp out at Ranchester on the night prior to our six-day tour. By the time I reached Sheridan, however, I was starting to feel uncomfortable, so I got a motel room and plugged in the heating pad.

While driving west on I-90 the next morning, I saw early-bird cyclists headed back east on the service roads. It pleased me that many tourers would be ahead of me, out of the way. I had never ridden with a pack this large. I checked in at the high school near Ranchester and was issued a colorful shirt and helmet cover. My backpack with personal gear, tent, and foam pad was deposited with other duffel bags for loading onto a gigantic Army transport vehicle. I joined a half dozen other late starters. We rode east, bantering a bit, nervously checking out others' home towns, history, and experience. Very soon we were on a dirt road, off course, laughing at our mutual inability to correctly interpret the tour guide symbols. The mistake was quickly corrected. We were now very human and we were friends.

People from all over the United States gathered for this tour. There were six couples on tandems. Groups from Kansas City, Salt Lake City, and Denver participated, but I only knew two riders from Colorado. Annie Lombard was one. In the afternoon, when the winds picked up, coming unpredictably from the southeast, she and I drafted each other for the final miles into Buffalo.

I pitched my tiny tent under a tree near the high school tennis courts. A young lady had been watching me organize my possessions.

"Hi," I said.

"Hi," she replied. "I was just interested in how you arranged your camp. You are in the shade, on high ground which will drain, out of the foot traffic pattern, and have your own personal bike rack and laundry hanger."

"It's taken a long time to learn, through countless errors."

Her name was Rebecca Shaw. Unlike most of us, she had a helmet cover with a red cross on a white field. She was riding as medical support. Her home was in Laramie, where she worked as a nurse in a hospital emergency room.

"How do you deal with all that bad stuff in your job—the blood, pain, and death?" I asked. "I know a couple of other ladies who do the same thing. I'm convinced that they have to be very special people."

"I suppose no one gets totally hardened to it. Something new is always happening, but I think I have learned to be objective, and still be a caring person."

As we rode west out of Buffalo the next morning, I was joined by a young man from the Utah contingency. We were on a gentle upgrade which was no real problem, but he cranked at a pace too fast for me. He soon mumbled an unnecessary apology and burst ahead. I was to learn later that he was probably the most powerful rider on the tour. Our road entered a canyon and then pitched upward significantly. We were headed toward Powder River Pass and, unlike most of Colorado's big divides, the steepest part of the route was at the bottom. I did not do very well on this portion. There was no discomfort in my shoulder while riding, but I was tiring quickly. Rest the night before had been fitful. Every time I moved the least bit in my sleeping bag, I woke up from the soreness and Rice Krispie sounds due to my accident. One benefit: the new medicine cured tendinitis in my elbows, permanently.

It got cloudy as we climbed. Then it started to drizzle and the temperature dropped. People left the road to put on rain gear. I had a decent jacket and trousers for this exposure, but no full-finger gloves or shoe covers. A few miles from the summit, our tour directors had erected a blue plastic tarpaulin adjacent to the sag vehicles. A number of bikers stopped to cower under this protection, huddling away from the edges where sheets of water spilled. The truck cabs were full of people. My eyes met those of another older cyclist standing across from me. I wondered if he could see the concern in my countenance which I seemed to detect in his. I am no stranger to hypothermia and we were right on the verge. There seemed to be nothing to do but push on.

I finally topped the pass and rode down as fast as safety would allow. Visibility was very poor and the road surface slick. It continued to rain. My goal was one of two lodges reported to be ahead. Many others had the same idea, to find a fireside and get warm.

We ate chili and drank hot chocolate and laughed noisily while our outer clothing cooked on the stone facade over a huge fireplace. The owner of the inn graciously tolerated the desecration of his lounge by steaming attire, thankful for the business. I was in the place for over two hours before riding in the dry to Ten Sleep, Wyoming.

On our third day, I elected to ride twenty-eight miles to Worland for breakfast, because the restaurant which I peered into at Ten Sleep was bursting with bodies. The ride was cool and pleasant through arid rolling country. A few miles from Worland, a tandem went whistling by me on a downgrade. Enchanted by the country, I had not seen it gaining on me, and it startled me. A tandem on the flat or downhill can really shame a single rider for speed. About ten minutes later, I saw congestion on the road ahead. Automobile traffic was stopped on a bridge. I rode up fast and saw a bicycle lying flat on the paving. Rebecca was kneeling by the bridge railing, cradling the torso of another rider in her arms. I stopped, leaned my bike against the rail and knelt down beside them.

"How were you able to get here so quickly?" I asked.

"I was riding along with her," Rebecca replied. "She's my best friend." Rebecca gulped and choked and fought for control. Her objectivity was now being sorely tested. She adjusted her grip on the downed rider, who had tears streaming down her face. "Amber, could you drink some water?" Blood was seeping through Amber Travsky's clothing, on her hip and near her shoulder. I leaned forward to grasp Amber's blouse and gently pull it away. Her shoulder was a mess. I glanced at the broom-finished concrete slab which had abraded her and made a wry face, squinting back at Rebecca.

"I'm sorry. I didn't mean . . ." I said.

"I know. It's O.K.," Rebecca said. "Help's on the way. See if you can gather her bike."

I walked back on the bridge to retrieve Amber's bicycle. Both caps on the handlebars had blown out from the collision, but her bike seemed to roll all right and appeared to have no serious damage. A driver in a parked pickup motioned me over. "I saw the whole thing," he said. "I don't know what caused her to go down."

"It could have been that rock on the paving." I pointed.

"Don't think so. She just appeared to faint."

I walked back to the ladies, rolling the tiny bicycle. Amber was sitting up. I asked her if she had eaten any breakfast. She could not remember.

It was later ascertained that Amber had acquired a concussion and a cracked collar bone in exchange for her lost skin. When told by the examining doctor that her touring was finished, an attending nurse pulled Amber aside and whispered, "Get another opinion." The second doctor told her, in effect, that there was not much he could do for her, but more bicycling could do her no harm if she could tolerate the pain. The next day, Amber was again on her bike, riding with the group. My own shoulder pain became very insignificant.

We were in Thermopolis by noon. I chose to forego a soak in the hot springs, which probably would have helped me to relax. On Wednesday, we covered a 52-mile stretch to Meeteetse, where we were greeted with a barbecue, beer, dancing, and revelry. Annie was annoyed somewhat by the overzealous attentions of a companion from Denver, so I walked her "home" that evening to her spot in the high school gym and retreated to my tent. On awakening, I detected water on and in my sleeping bag. It was raining. I packed my belongings, wet, and prepared for the daily ride. No one likes to ride in the rain. It is particularly tough to *start* a ride when it is raining. But it was a new experience for me to have companions who were faced with a like problem. It sure made it easier. Misery loves company.

As we rode north, then curved east toward Greybull, the rain abated. It turned out to be a lovely day for a relaxed ride following the Greybull River. There was even less traffic on this out-of-the-way road than elsewhere in the state. We continued on to Shell and set up camp in the bright sun, drying wet equipment on volleyball nets. Our last day put us on Granite Pass, where my performance was anything but stellar. I was exhausted from lack of sound sleep. The ride over was cloudy and we could see very little of the surrounding peaks. I encountered Rebecca and her friend. "How's it going, Amber? How are your hurts?" I asked.

"Pretty good. I'm a bit rank 'cause I can't shower. The water jets are murder on my road rash."

The last miles, the drop off the pass, tested everyone again with fog and cold. We had to ride very carefully because trucks and autos were descending slower than we were. It was very pleasant to hop into my car, drive to Sheridan, and jump into a hot motel shower. Despite my belief that a bicycle tour without some adversity would be dull indeed, I was ready for a rest. I would have been in dour shape for Ride the Rockies.

Although the RAW riders did not always have an unobstructed view of the magnificent countryside, this had been a trip to reward the senses. I was proud of the manner in which cyclists from diverse environments met this challenge with good humor. Many had never encountered a mountain road before.

In July, I led another club day-ride to Evergreen, up in the mountains. It was called "Bob's Bad Person Ride." On the back of each cyclist, I pinned the name of an infamous someone from literature or history. Each rider was to "identify" himself by querying his companions, somewhat like the game "Twenty Questions." This was supposed to take everyone's mind off the climb up the service road in Mount Vernon Canyon. Annie and Carol were on this jaunt also, Carol now as a member. When we stopped for lunch in Kittredge, I received some heat from a couple of ladies who complained about their new identity. Undaunted, I followed the pack back toward Morrison, unable still to keep up with Carol, even on the downgrade. At the end of this ride, I learned that one of our participants had been struck by a car. I questioned Annie about this later. She had not witnessed the incident either.

The bicycle accidents continued. Bud's daughter fell and suffered head injuries requiring extensive rehabilitation. She was not wearing a helmet.

My next door neighbor, Dick Olde, made a routine little turn on new paving in Vail. He fell and thought he had a sprain in his leg. It was a fracture requiring surgery.

Returning from an outing with the D.B.T.C., I was greeted with Anne's usual query, "How was your ride?"

"OK, but I saw another accident. I'm beginning to feel like the Kiss of Death."

"That's nonsense and you know it. What happened?"

"We were on the Bear Creek bike path, almost finished with our ride. Two of our club members went around me fast and then yelled at a little kid walking ahead. The kid turned around to see what was coming, then jumped back right into the path of a biker coming the other way."

"Was anyone hurt?"

"The little kid lay on the ground and yelled a lot but he wasn't really hurt. The biker went over his handlebars and was cut up pretty bad. I rode on to get the car, drove back and took him home. His bike was wrecked, too."

"That was nice of you."

"I'm not sure his wife thought so. To her it probably looked like I was the culprit, had hit him with my car. Actually, our own riders in the club caused this accident. They should know better."

"How so?"

"They performed just well enough to be considered blameless, but they weren't really very thoughtful. Shouting their terse 'on your left,' they expected a youngster to remove himself with zero reaction time.

That's asking too much of anyone, let alone a little kid. Too many gunners are blasting around a path as if it were their own personal time trial course. It gives cyclists a bad reputation. The joggers, skateboarders, and old codgers walking their dogs have a right to be there too."

Arch called me early one morning, "Are you going to be home for awhile? I have to come to Lakewood and thought I would stop by."

"I have an arbitration hearing. I won't be here after ten minutes."

"No problem. Catch you later."

When I came home that night, there was a brand new mountain bike in my garage. I conferred with Anne, called Arch and asked, "What are you about?"

"I figured I had better get you off the streets before you kill yourself," he responded. "Now, I know you will get all uptight about this, but just accept the thing and have some fun." I had been helping Arch with a remodel of his farmhouse off and on for over a year and the guilt must have gotten to him.

"I'm not sure I'm ready to ride on dirt."

"You won't play golf."

"Golf is for old men. I don't feel old if I stay away from reflective objects. I'll try the bike. Thank you." Arch is much younger than I am.

I had not received his gift very graciously and I agonized over the prospect of equipping and maintaining three bicycles. Finally, I took Arch's choice into the dealer and exchanged it for a larger model which fit me. Then I took my new machine out for a test ride on the Clear Creek Greenbelt. I was trying to ride it like a teenager, smoking down the dirt paths, hopping rocks and ditches. I charged up a little ramp toward a wooden footbridge which was a few inches above the earth. I pulled up hard to jump the bike. We didn't make it. The front wheel hit the deck head on and I fell over to the side, a pedal gouging my shin. I called Arch.

"Does this bike come with an insurance policy? It took me twelve years to hurt myself on the road bike and this mother jumps up to bite me on the first ride."

I bought some toe clips, a back rack, two bottle cages, another pump, and I decided to be more careful. I tried the mountain bike on a mountain road. On gravel, it was much more forgiving than my touring bike would be. I tried two forty-mile rides on paving with the club and they just about did me in, as I tried to keep up with the crowd. I quickly perceived that the mountain bike would be no good for touring, but it had other charms. I threw it in the back of my car and just left it there, like a lifeboat, ready for a quick escape any time. I rode it on many little excursions with the Golden Cycling Seniors. They used nothing but mountain bikes, but seldom on difficult rough terrain.

Then Arch called me. "I haven't seen you around for awhile," he said. "You know, there is still work to be done up here. You haven't finished the painting you started." I could hear sounds of debauchery in the background. It was the monthly meeting of Arch's Gold Hill Investment Club. "I told the guys here that you still had work to do and Jim Bodin said, 'That ingrate son-of-a-bitch, you gave him the bike too soon.'"

In mid-November, the *Denver Post* ran an article about a triathlete who was hit head-on by a Chevrolet Blazer while training on his bicycle west of Loveland Pass. A witness reported that the driver of the vehicle stopped, went over to peer at the injured cyclist, and then left the scene. After calling St. Anthony Hospital to find out if Larry Palubicki could receive visitors, I knocked on his door and entered. His sister had traveled from Wisconsin to be with him. Larry had broken ribs, his face was black and blue, and his jaw was wired. I asked him if the driver had been passing another car. He did not remember, but stated that the vehicle came way over on his own side of the highway to blow him off the shoulder. He then received a phone call and I could see that it was very difficult for him to converse. I talked with his sister for a bit and left. She reported that many cyclists had called or stopped by to express their concern.

Just before Christmas came the worst news of all. Carol Gosline's brother, Don Feige, a Peace Corps volunteer, was killed while cycling in Florida. He was hit by a truck. The year of 1990 was not kind to bicyclists.

It was not a startling discovery that riding a two-wheeled machine could be a hazardous endeavor. I knew there was risk. But I was bothered by the rash of incidents which was a reminder of my own mortality. How could I have traveled so many miles in unfamiliar territory without trauma? Was Arch correct in steering me toward golf? I was on another downer, accentuated no doubt by my propensity to be SAD during winter, a possible victim of Seasonal Affective Disorder. The prospect of war did not help. I was reacting poorly to any sort of setback, falling into a pit of depression, until one day when I visited a local copy shop. On the wall was a poster which attracted my attention. On it was the caption "LOST DOG." Below that was a picture of a forlorn looking hound. Under that it stated "3 legs, blind in left eye, missing right ear, tail broken, recently castrated . . . Answers to name of 'Lucky.'"

I laughed out loud at that poster. It put things into perspective since I had a great deal in common with Lucky. I made a copy of the message and shared it with friends. A few started to address me by the nickname. Anne, of course, had long attested to my good fortune.

Can we learn from Lucky, who plays the game of life with indomitable spirit? We have no choice whether to enter the contest, the referees are not always fair, sometimes the rules change, our equipment may be faulty, and we have less chance of coming in first than winning the lottery. We can plan and pray, toil and sweat, exhibiting skill, creativity, patience, daring, perseverance. We can temper our moves with caution. Yet, a little luck would come in handy. Some will have it. Some won't.

Lately, I have come to yearn again for the joys of a long bicycle tour in the big open spaces, where its safe. You will not have to ponder long to determine where I want to go next. It cannot be a ride to Hawaii. A long snorkel just ain't gonna work. I want to romance Alaska some.

Former residents of our 49th state have warned me about this trip. They are concerned that I might be eaten by a bear, so they suggest that I have a companion. I suppose there is some merit in their recommendation. Any exponent of the buddy system knows there is a fifty-fifty chance that the carnivore will eat one's buddy, not oneself. You are welcome to join me. I will tote the olives. With any luck at all, you will end up as a chewor, not a chewee.

CHAPTER 20

THE BEST RIDE

My paternal grandfather, Harvey, was a taciturn man. However, if you could get him going, he was a wealth of information. His happy discourses would usually occur after dinner when he was enjoying his daily cigar. Since the cigar was more a chew than a smoke, Grand-dad's comments were interrupted frequently by an accurate spit through a screened window on the cabin front porch. As long as I am alive, the rust on that screen will be preserved. He talked about trips to "the park" from Sioux City in his Stutz or Marmon. The trip might take a week because they were towed through enough muddy bogs by horse teams to make the choice of attempting the journey by auto suspect. Heck, I could ride a bike from Sioux City quicker—now.

Grand-dad told us about fishing trips to Squeaky Bob's sod-thatched cabins north of Grand Lake and watching convict chain gangs build Fall River Road to the Continental Divide. He talked about Jack Moomaw and Johnny Adams. And he talked about Bailey.

Bailey Leatherman helped to rebuild our cabin when the drafty old log structure was acquired in about 1931 by the right of eminent domain to improve the look of Rocky Mountain National Park. The park service was going to burn the house. In a hasty effort to save it, my folks bought new land, disassembled the cabin, numbered the logs, trucked them down the road, and let Bailey and his cronies have at it. They rebuilt the place, better than it was.

Bailey lived in Rand, Colorado, on Highway 125. He and his wife Dolly ran the hotel there. The hotel was the only two-story structure on Rand's "strip," which was one block long. Every so often a lonesome traveler would stop at the Rand Hotel, but if he really wanted action he would go up to Walden to watch haircuts or an oil change. It was a hard, simple life for Bailey and Dolly. The story goes that in his wilder-oated days, Bailey got a hankering to travel back east and observe life in the big city. "Back east" and "big city" in Bailey's mind meant Omaha or Kansas City. I'm not sure that he discovered the blessings of Chicago but he scraped up his savings and journeyed to the two other cattle centers. It was a long trip by train and bus. The urban bustle was a shocking education for a man steeped in the life of the West. Bailey endured the trip back to Denver and Rand, stomped into the hotel, grabbed his .30-.30, climbed on a horse, and reined it over sandy bluffs to the banks of the Illinois River. He looked down at the meandering dinky brown ribbon of a stream where wily trout hid in foam-flecked corners under the willows. He looked up at the ridges of Owl Mountain sweeping northwest and east from a talus-filled scar. He watched a herd of elk ramble through the brush and disappear into the aspen trees on a gentle slope above. Bailey raised his frame from the saddle and stood in the stirrups. He threw out his arms and said, "Thank God for a place where a man can stretch."

You don't have to convince me, Bailey. That's where I want to be, too—the *big* country. That's where it all happens. Now I don't want to upset anyone. There are beautiful places in every state of the Union. I know that. Please be at ease and forgive me. I'm from the West.

The West is immense and it has mountains, huge mountains, stringing ranges of them. Crossing the ranges are the passes and that's where the best bike rides are. Any ride over a respectable pass is worth ten rides in the flat countryside and fifty jaunts down a city bike path. When you blast down from the high mountains you are alive. But you have to pay for the privilege. You have to ride up the things.

I have heard of a tour "service" which will haul you and your bike to the top for a fee. I think it is in Hawaii. This is a disgrace, criminal. If I ever catch you doing this, I will bite your tires.

Tourists unfamiliar with the West are astonished at the immensity of it. Many do not realize that all six of the New England states plus three-fourths of New York State would fit in an area the size of Colorado.

Look at the maps of Colorado in the back of this book. They show the main highways. The heavier lines are routes I have traveled by bicycle. The numbers on one map indicate the sequence of passes crossed.

Motorists crossing the Nebraska or Kansas border are often distressed that in order to reach Colorado's "purple mountain majesties" eloquently depicted by Katherine Lee Bates, they must first traverse miles and miles of rolling grassland. Through these eastern plains are three heavily lined routes, which indicate the beginning of major bicycle tours. All are safe, smoothly paved highways with broad shoulders. They are relatively untouched by cyclists. The helter-skelter routes west of Denver and the other front range cities provide the real bicycling action—in the foothills and mountains which cover only two-thirds of the state. Roads here are mostly of high quality with reasonable shoulders.

There isn't any question about the location of the absolute best bicycle ride in the world. It's over Trail Ridge Road in Colorado. It is the world's highest paved continuous highway. You don't just cross a ridge and slide down. You wander up and down and around in the tundra for miles, with the Mummy Range and Never Summer Range and Horseshoe Park and Forest Canyon feeding your soul. This is the Big Daddy of bicycle rides. Come try it. But remember, this is my game so I make the rules. You have to leave from your house. If you live in Cheyenne, bully for you. If you live in Jacksonville, tough beans.

I have found some other great rides which don't put you at high altitude. I have mentioned them elsewhere. I know there are thousands more. Some of my friends tour in Spain and Scotland. I have no desire to leave the United States. There are so many places here yet to visit. In case you haven't discovered it by now, there is one other map at the back of this book. It is of the United States, which have hardly been touched by me. Anyone who says that I never gave some of the states a fair shake is certainly correct. Look at Arizona, Wisconsin, and Michigan for example. I just popped in and then right out. Sorry, gang. I'd like to take another shot at it, but this time without the rules. I just might arrive there first in a car.

I won't necessarily avoid the cities. City riding is fine if you know what you are getting into. You should have more than a map, some real knowledge of the layout and the temperament of the people. Consider what an unknowing tourer would face if he came riding into Denver from Kansas. He would enter Aurora onto East Colfax Avenue from I-70 or the service roads. Colfax is one of the longest city streets in the nation. His map would tell him that he could stay on Colfax clear through the city and suburbs. It would be a nasty ride for twenty-four miles, one which few local bikers would attempt, a high-risk route.

I have biked in the suburban areas of L.A. and Chicago with aplomb. I have been through three Portlands with no problem. I was confused in downtown Rochester, New York, by street repairs; I got on the wrong road in Rochester, New Hampshire, because I was not paying attention. But I was comfortable in both cities, as well as Missoula, Des Moines, Buffalo, Rapid City, Hartford, Mobile, and Washington, D.C. I was scared in Minneapolis. My two-day biking buddy in Kansas, Terry Ferstle, rode through the Bronx without incident, but he was uneasy. Your comfort and safety can depend on the time of day, the weather, your own skill, and the awareness of the natives. Luck is good, judgment is better.

I avoided Cleveland, Boston, New York City, Philadelphia, Atlanta. It seemed to be the proper thing to do. I knew nothing about these cities. On a Sunday evening, I rode through Baltimore on Truck Route 1 trying to find a motel after a terribly long and windy ride from Marsh Creek State Park in Pennsylvania. It turned out to be a 120-mile day, ending in Elkridge. I was tired and hungry and somewhat concerned for my well-being. In retrospect, it was a memorable journey through black Americana on North Avenue and Monroe Street. The sounds were marvelous—live jazz, boom boxes, shouts, the unnerving blare of overtaking fire trucks. Some folks stared at me. I might have been scorned if in a stretch limo, but they were passively delighted by my touring bike and its impediments. I pulled alongside a huge black dude stopped on his Harley at a traffic signal. "That's a fine looking bike," I said. He turned his head slowly to appraise me and my equipment. He squeezed on the grips and muscles rippled in his back and arms. He took a long, hard, penetrating look. I was petrified.

"Thank you," he said.

You would not believe the images I have stored in my head. My built-in camcorder has no zoom lens, but it didn't cost anything and my helmet serves as the case. My camera takes still pictures and movies. I can play back the tape and see nervous ducks rising out of a slough, arroyos, tunnels of conifers, kids waving, the black soil of Minnesota, and snow-capped peaks on the horizon. I can see lightning-split dark clouds, waves of grass in the plains, lily-filled ponds, the five-mile bridge across the mouth of the Columbia, and thousands of cattle staring at me. The cattle chew slowly and I say, "Hi, cows." I expect the cattle are mostly all dead now, but I am still alive, rolling around with this album in my brain.

You see, I use my camcorder to photo everything I own, kinda like you do for insurance purposes. For a brief moment I have owned all of this stuff, just like Bailey "owned" every square inch of North Park in spite of his meager life style. Neither Bailey nor I made the purchase with dollars. We had no deed recorded at the county courthouse. Bailey "bought" all the land his eyes could survey. He established title with sweat and devotion, but he eventually gave it all back. In my case, I paid for each exquisite view with every downstroke on the cranks. It was mine. I owned it, but only for a few minutes, until I was over the ridge. Then I had to give it back, to you, or anyone else who will guard it. Katherine Bates would never have wished to own all this beauty, I am positive. She wanted to share. In Bali they say, "Only the Gods can own land. We humans only borrow it for awhile."

No one can steal the pictures from me. You may never collect your own gallery if you don't get cracking. You cannot copy my tapes. It doesn't work that way.

Get started. You can ride your bike or motorcycle. You may want to get off and walk to see the really good places. With the proper frame of mind, you can even go in your car. It's an attitude, not a marathon. However, you might as well get used to climbing the hills. When you journey to your eternal reward, the Great Freeway in the Sky, you will have to crank uphill to get there, too. Not to worry. The big eighteen-wheelers will pull way over to give you room. The cars will honk lightly and give you a thumbs up—after they pass. Some will stop to hand you your parts which are still falling off. They might even offer you an icy cold brew. There won't be any delivery vans, dump trucks, RV's, or pickups. These guys will be going down, to the bad place, dealing with their own private perdition, the logging trucks.

CHAPTER 21

EPILOGUE

There is an abundance of "I" on the preceding pages. The personal pronoun is difficult to avoid when the events described are mostly solo adventures. Nevertheless, I apologize.

Jim Konkel and I were hunting in the weedy draws of western Kansas some years ago. It was too warm for good hunting. We hadn't seen a pheasant all morning and we were beginning to suspect that the species was extinct. Jim parked the van to prepare lunch. His lunches were legend, often the high point of the day. We feasted leisurely on cold fried chicken, cheese, deviled eggs, and hot peppers. I drained my wine glass and announced, "Now I am going to shoot a pheasant," and stepped to the ground. I took three strides into the ditch adjacent and a handsome rooster burst from the cover right at my feet. He had been hiding during our entire repast. I wasn't ready. You never are. The creature came up so close that I had time to recover and bring up my shotgun. I fired and the bird fell.

Jim peered from the window of his vehicle, laughing at my astonishment and drawled, "Dizzy Dean said, 'It ain't braggin' if you can do it.'"

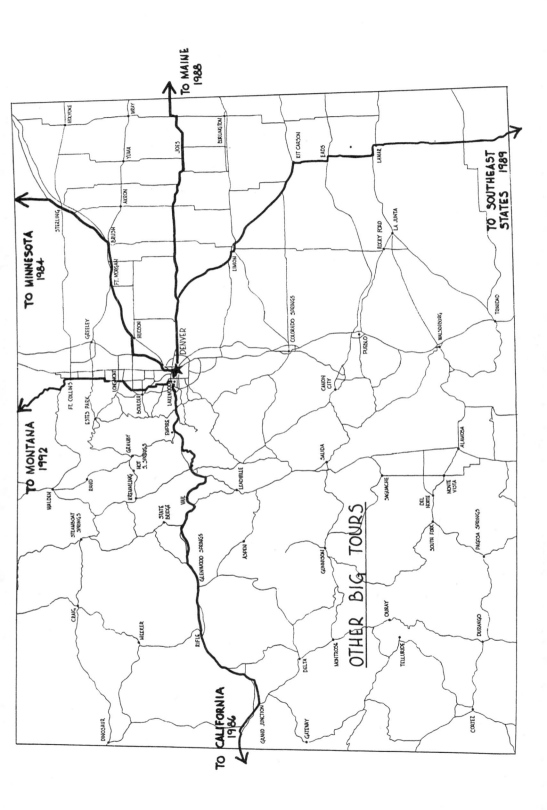

TO MAINE 1988

TO SOUTHEAST STATES 1989

TO MINNESOTA 1984

TO MONTANA 1992

TO CALIFORNIA 1986

OTHER BIG TOURS

HOLYOKE
WRAY
YUMA
JOES
BURLINGTON
AKRON
STERLING
KIT CARSON
EADS
BRUSH
LAMAR
FT. MORGAN
ROCKY FORD
LA JUNTA
HUDSON
LIMON
GREELEY
COLORADO SPRINGS
WALSENBURG
DENVER
TRINIDAD
FT. COLLINS
PUEBLO
LONGMONT
CAÑON CITY
BOULDER
LAKEWOOD
ESTES PARK
EMPIRE
GRANBY
HOT SULPHUR SPRINGS
SALIDA
ALAMOSA
RAND
KREMMLING
LEADVILLE
SAGUACHE
WALDEN
VAIL
STATE BRIDGE
DEL NORTE
MONTE VISTA
STEAMBOAT SPRINGS
GUNNISON
SOUTH FORK
PAGOSA SPRINGS
ASPEN
CRAIG
GLENWOOD SPRINGS
MEEKER
OURAY
DURANGO
DINOSAUR
RIFLE
DELTA
MONTROSE
TELLURIDE
GRAND JUNCTION
GATEWAY
CORTEZ

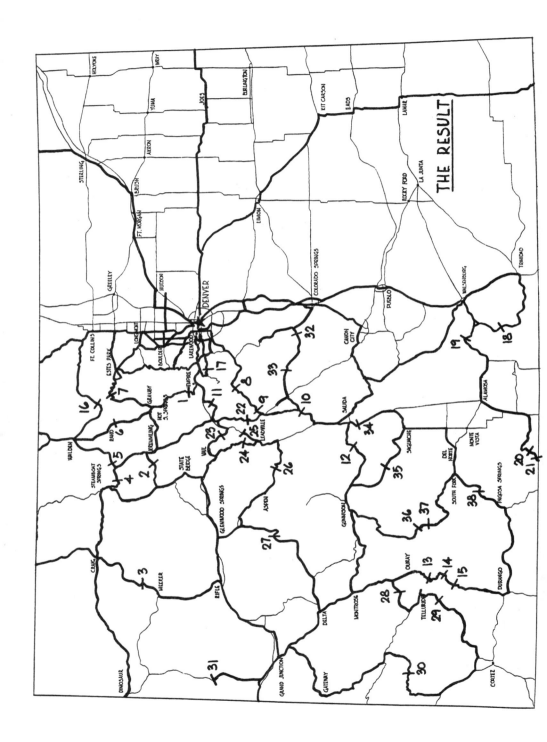

THE RESULT

Passes Bicycled Outside of Colorado

1979   The Rim, Wyoming (also 1980)
       Gilmore Divide, Idaho
       Lost Trail, Idaho

1980   Flaming Gorge, Utah
       Craig, Wyoming (also 1992)
       Butte, Montana
       Sherman, Washington
       Wauconda, Washington
       Loup Loup, Washington
       Washington, Washington
       Rainy, Washington

1984   Red River, New Mexico (start from Antonito, Colorado)

1986   Loa, Utah

1988   Snowy Range, Wyoming (start from Laramie, Wyoming)

1990   Powder River, Wyoming (start from Ranchester, Wyoming, in the RAW)
       Granite, Wyoming

1992   Togwotee, Wyoming

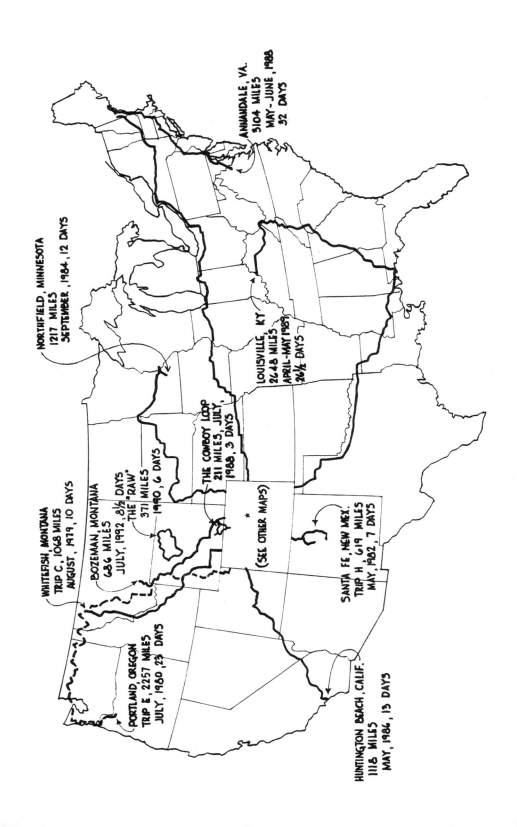

ANNANDALE, VA.
5104 MILES
MAY-JUNE, 1988
32 DAYS

NORTHFIELD, MINNESOTA
1217 MILES
SEPTEMBER, 1984, 12 DAYS

LOUISVILLE, KY
2648 MILES
APRIL-MAY 1987
24½ DAYS

WHITEFISH, MONTANA
TRIP C, 1068 MILES
AUGUST, 1979, 10 DAYS

BOZEMAN, MONTANA
686 MILES
JULY, 1992, 8½ DAYS

THE "RAW"
371 MILES
1990, 6 DAYS

THE COWBOY LOOP
211 MILES, JULY,
1988, 3 DAYS

(SEE OTHER MAPS)

SANTA FE, NEW MEX.
TRIP H, 619 MILES
MAY, 1982, 7 DAYS

PORTLAND, OREGON
TRIP E, 2257 MILES
JULY, 1980, 23 DAYS

HUNTINGTON BEACH, CALIF.
1118 MILES
MAY, 1986, 13 DAYS

INDEX